MARINE DECISIONS UNDER UNCERTAINTY

MARINE DECISIONS UNDER UNCERTAINTY

by

John W. Devanney III

MASSACHUSETTS INSTITUTE OF TECHNOLOGY

Sea Grant Project Office

Cambridge, Massachusetts 02139

Report No. MITSG 71-7
Index No. 71-107-Nte

Published by

CORNELL MARITIME PRESS, INC.
Cambridge, Maryland 21613

ACKNOWLEDGMENT

This text was prepared under the auspices of the Ocean Engineering Program at the Massachusetts Institute of Technology. It is also the final report of the M.I.T. Sea Grant Program 1970-71 project element "OE/Marine Transportation." The preparation of these materials was supported in part by a grant from the National Sea Grant Program, GH-88, in part by funds from the Henry L. and Grace Doherty Charitable Foundation, Inc., and in part by M.I.T. funds.

The materials contained in this book were assembled and written by Professor John W. Devanney, III and were developed in conjunction with a new subject, "Marine Decision Making Under Uncertainty" offered during the Spring Term, 1971. The text was also used for a Special Summer Program presented in June 1971.

Alfred H. Keil, Director
Sea Grant Program

November 1971

PREFACE

The objective of this monograph is to facilitate the
application of Bayesian decision theory in the marine industry.
The author's experience in dealing with various parts of the
marine industry indicated that people at two separate levels
had to be addressed if a much broader and more systematic application of modern decision theory in marine operations could
be effected.

Practicing marine decision-makers have to be introduced
to the basic concepts of decision-making under uncertainty at an
elementary level in the context of problems with which they
are familiar. Analysts who have the background need illustra-
tive examples which bring the full force of these ofttimes
powerful techniques to bear on some of the more challenging
problems facing the marine investor and operators. As a
result, the book is more than a little dichotomous.

The first three chapters constitute an elementary introduction to decisions under uncertainty, Bayesian decision theory and
dynamic programming respectively. They assume no prior knowledge
of these techniques. In these chapters only the presentation is
original and sometimes not even that. Chapter 1 is adapted from
Ronald Howard's class notes entitled "The Used Car Buyer" and
Chapter 2 leans heavily on Raiffa's eminently readable "Decision
Analysis" which is highly recommended as companion reading.

The final three chapters apply these techniques to a hopefully
representative spectrum of marine problems involving substantial
uncertainties. These chapters presuppose an increasing level of
probabilistic sophistication. In particular, Chapters 5 and 6
assume some familiarity with continuous random variables and
density functions. However, the arguments used in these latter
chapters are basically repeated applications of the same simple
principles developed in the first three. Therefore, it is hoped
that a reader without any training in probability will be able to
follow the gist of the reasoning. Conversely, readers familiar with
probability, Bayesian decision theory or dynamic programming should
skip the respective introductory chapters or tarry there only long
enough to pick up the author's notational idiosyncracies before
moving on to the applications.

Chapter 4 is directed at the alternatives facing those decisionmakers who operate in the ship charter markets, both owners and charterers. The chapter begins with a study of the vessel employment decisions facing an owner who already has a ship--whether or not to accept the present charter rates and, if so, for what length of charter. Once we have developed methodology for generating chartering decisions which are consistent with the owner's feelings about the uncertain future of the market, it is a relatively simple matter to broaden our horizon a bit and address the problem of whether or not the owner should invest in a ship. Chapter 4 concludes with a brief treatment of the problem facing the combined owner-charterer such as the large oil company and develops methodology for comparing alternative mixes of own ships, long term charters, and short term charters.

Chapter 5 is devoted to marine hardware maintenance problems. This chapter is based on the premise that typically the decisionmaker not only does not know when a component will fail but also he does not even know how reliable the component is in the sense of knowing the parameters which govern the failure process. He cannot, for example, be sure what the mean time between failures is of a new power plant with which he has very limited operating experience. Chapter 5 addresses this problem by starting with a situation in which these two types of uncertainties are related in an extremely simple manner, boiler tube replacement; and then moves to the general problem of how one might design maintenance and replacement policies when one has limited failure data on the components in question.

Chapter 6 addresses search and exploration problems at sea. Once again the underlying idea is that the decisionmaker not only does not know where the object of his search is, but also he does not know how good his sensors are in locating whatever he is searching for. Bayesian thinking is applied to this set of problems in the context of retrieval of a lost object and then in the context of exploration for offshore petroleum resources.

Various members of the marine systems group at M.I.T. share responsibility for the applications described in Chapters 3 through 6. In particular, Alan Woodyard programmed the vessel employment routine while Joe Lassiter developed some of the more important properties of the hyperPoisson. I am indebted to General Dynamics/Electric Boat for supporting the original work on the sub production scheduling program and to Cruiser-Destroyer Force Atlantic for supporting the development of the maintenance algorithms. Computation was accomplished at the M.I.T. Information Processing Center and the writing and development of the text, as well as the course upon which it is based, was financed by the National Sea Grant Foundation and the Grace L. Doherty Foundation through the M.I.T. Sea Grant Office.

TABLE OF CONTENTS

MARINE DECISIONS UNDER UNCERTAINTY

CHAPTER 1

AN INTRODUCTORY EXAMPLE

1.1 PREAMBLE

All decision-makers face varying degrees of uncertainty. However, few executives confront uncertainties of the type and magnitude facing the marine investor and operator. Operating at sea has always been an inherently risky business attracting only the bold or the desperate. And, if it is less risky now with respect to bodily survival, it is hardly less risky with respect to economic survival. For example, the independent tanker owner-- and his customer, the charterer--operate in a commodity market the magnitude of whose price fluctuations is unheard of in any other financial arena. The spot tanker rate can vary by a factor of seven or eight in a matter of months depending on the vagaries of oil finds and the policies and whims of less than completely stable governments. The owner's capital is tied up in a small number of very large units. Despite technological progress, he is still sensitive to wind and fog and operator error in a unique way. The loss of a single unit will involve losses and liabilities of tens of millions of dollars.

Or consider the case of the man who would tap the ocean floor for petroleum or minerals. The offshore operator immediately faces exploration costs which are not only ten times greater than their upland counterparts, but which are far less predictable as well. Further, the information he obtains from the same experiments is generally of a much lower quality leaving him with much greater uncertainties at the point where he must decide to drill or mine. Finally, the costs of such production operations are an order of magnitude greater and far less predictable than they are on land. Yet, mineral and petroleum exploration and development on land is regarded by landlubbers as an extremely risky business indeed.

In short, the essence of marine decision-making is the juggling of uncertainties, the balancing of risk versus return.

1

Despite this fact, the systematic treatment of uncertainty has received little attention in marine practice or the marine literature.* One result of this lack of attention is that the marine decision-maker finds that the set of decisions to which he can usefully apply quantitative analysis is quite limited. The resulting attitude is concisely expressed in the sometimes skeptical, sometimes derogatory, and sometimes plaintive query: "How can you analyze what you cannot predict?" This book is an attempt to answer this perfectly reasonable question.

This book will suggest a systematic scheme for thinking about marine decisions in which the outcomes cannot be predicted. In very rough terms, the suggested analysis requires that you, the decision-maker,

1) Accept a certain small set of rules or axioms as to what constitutes "rational" decision-making under uncertainty--a set of axioms that you want your decisions to be consistent with, a set of axioms which I will attempt to persuade you make sense;

2) Having done so, we will be able to develop procedures for quantitatively assessing

    a) *your* judgments about the likelihood of the events which may affect the outcome of your choices,

    b) how well *you* like the consequences that may result for the various courses of action open to you;

3) Finally, we will develop procedures for synthesizing the judgments and values revealed in 2) to obtain decisions which are consistent with these judgments and values and the basic postulates concerning rational decision-making.

---

*Important exceptions to this statement include references 10, 11, and 21.

Needless to say, despite the somewhat dramatic introductory paragraph, not all marine decisions are worth the trouble. In many cases, your decisions can be made without a lot of fuss. Either your best choice is clear to you without much analysis or the decision is not important enough to be worth the effort. Occasionally, however, you will find yourself in situations with obviously important choices where it is not at all obvious which of a number of alternatives is consistent with your desires and your state of knowledge. It is to such decisions that this book is addressed.

We will begin our analysis of such decisions by examining in some detail a problem which is simple enough so that all the elements of decision-making under uncertainty can be clearly exhibited and complex enough so that it is not obvious at first glance just how the problem should be approached.

1.2 JOE, THE SECONDHAND BOAT BUYER*

A shipowner named Joe of our acquaintance is in the market for a used C4.** After surveying a number of brokers, he has found one such ship for one million dollars. The best deal he can get elsewhere is $1,100,000 for a fully found ship. Joe likes the looks of this particular ship and figures he will save $100,000 by buying it. Unfortunately, just as Joe is about to close the deal, he overhears the broker who has been serving him talking with another broker. His broker says, "This business is a tough racket. I have a buyer for that old C4, but the practices of our business prevent me from warning him that he may get stuck if he buys it." The other broker asks, "What do you mean?" Joe's broker replies, "I used to work for the company that built that ship. They built 20% of this class in a new yard where they were still having production troubles; those ships were lemons.

---

* A C4 is a moderately large general cargo ship built in the USA during the fifties.

**This problem and most of its description were originally developed by Ronald Howard in his classroom notes, "The Used Car Buyer." This material is being used through the permission of Professor Howard.

3

The other 80% of total production were pretty good ships; peaches, we used to call them." The other broker asks, "What is the difference between a 'lemon' and a 'peach?'" "Well," says Joe's man, "If we regard each ship as having 10 major subsystems, hull, power plant, fuel, electrical, etc.; the peaches all had a serious defect in only one of these 10 systems, but the lemons had serious defects in 6 out of 10 systems." The other broker replies, "Well, don't feel bad; maybe some ships didn't have any defects, or maybe the defects in this ship have already been fixed."

"No, that's just it," says Joe's broker. "Every ship of this age built by this company had either one or six defects in the ratio I mentioned, and I happen to know, because the previous operator was a friend of mine, that this particular ship has never been repaired." "If it is bothering you so much, why don't you tell the guy it's a lemon and forget about it?" says the other broker. "Ah," answers Joe's man, "that is the trouble. I personally don't know whether or not it is a lemon, and I am certainly not going to take the chance of losing a sale by worrying a customer unnecessarily." To which the other broker replies, "It's time for coffee."

We can imagine the state of our friend Joe. What seemed like a real bargain has turned into a potential nightmare. Joe's first reaction is to turn and flee, but he has the icy nerves required of a marine decision-maker and so soon regains his composure. Joe realizes that he would be foolish to forego the chance to buy the ship he thought he wanted, at this price, without good reason. He decides to call a nearby yard and get an estimate of what the possible repairs might cost. The yard reports that it costs about $40,000 to repair a single serious defect in one of a ship's major systems, but that if six defects were to be repaired the price for all six would be $200K.

Joe considers the possibilities open to him. He can buy the ship in which case his outcome is uncertain. If the C4 turns out to be a peach, then only one defect will develop and Joe will

4

have made a net gain of $60K--100K from buying the ship at a low
price less $40K for repairing the one defect. However, if the
ship should be a lemon, then Joe will lose $100K because it
will cost him $200,000 to repair the six defects to be found
in a lemon. If, on the other hand, he refuses to buy, then he
gains and loses nothing relative to where he stands now.

We can represent the structure of Joe's problem by drawing
a decision tree like that shown in Figure 1.1.

JOE'S ORIGINAL DECISION TREE

FIGURE 1.1

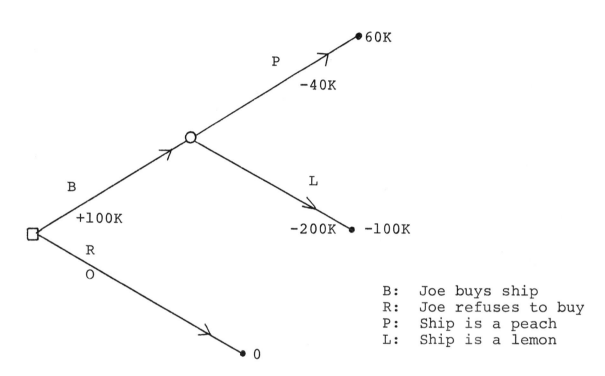

B: Joe buys ship
R: Joe refuses to buy
P: Ship is a peach
L: Ship is a lemon

In this diagram, the decision process moves from left to right
through time. Each branch or link represents some event in the
decision problem. We have used B to indicate the event of Joe's
buying the ship, and R to indicate his refusing it. P is the
event of the ship's ultimately turning out to be a peach, while
L is the event of the ship's being a lemon. Note that different
symbols are used for the junction point or node joining the B-R
branches and the modes joining the P-L branches. The ☐ is used

to indicate points in the decision tree where the decision-maker must decide on some act; the $\bigcirc$ is used for nodes where the branch to be taken is subject to chance rather than Joe's decision. We shall call these two types of intersections "decision nodes" and "chance nodes," respectively. In this example, Joe's only decision is whether to buy or refuse to buy; consequently, only the node joining the B-R branches requires an $\square$. The ultimate outcome as to whether the ship is a peach or a lemon is governed by chance and so the P-L branches are joined by an $\bigcirc$.

Generally, traversing each branch on the decision tree will bring some reward, positive or negative, to the decision-maker. We will write this reward under each branch. In Figure 1.1 we have written 100K under the branch labeled B to represent the immediate savings to Joe in buying the ship; 0 is written under the R branch because Joe will neither gain nor lose by refusing to buy. The numbers under the P and L branches refer to the cost of repairing a peach and lemon respectively. If the decision-maker follows a tree from its starting node to any of its tips, then he will experience some patterns of gains and losses according to the branches he actually traverses. The net gain of all such h traversals is written at each tip of the tree. Each tip may be designated by the sequence of branches that leads to it. Thus, in this case the tip BP is given the value $60K, the net gain in buying the ship and then finding that it is a peach. The tip BL corresponds to a loss of $100K from buying a lemon, while the tip R is evaluated at zero because the ship is refused. These three tips of the tree represent the three possible outcomes of this decision problem.

Naturally, Joe would like the outcome to be BP with a net gain of $60K but, after hearing the broker's conversation, he realizes that the likelihood of this outcome will be controlled by Nature rather than by himself, where "Nature" is just an anthropomorphic way of saying that Joe is not sure of the outcome. Following up on this anthropomorphism, we can think of Nature as playing a game with Joe as follows: In order to de-

6

cide whether to make Joe's ship a peach or a lemon, Nature
flips a coin in which the odds of a head are 8 out of 10. If
the coin comes up heads, Nature chooses a peach; if tails, a
lemon.

Joe is a confirmed horseplayer, so he has no trouble
thinking quantitatively about likelihoods. However, he has had
some difficulty keeping track of the myriad ways horseplayers
talk about their chances. He realizes that the expression "the
chances are four out of five," "eight out of ten" or "sixteen out
of twenty" all express the same likelihood. He has found it
expedient in thinking about his chances in horseracing to express all his odds relative to the same base, namely, the number 1.00. That is, he is in the habit of assigning a likelihood of 1.00 to events he is certain will happen and a likelihood of .00 to events he is certain will not happen. To an
event whose chances are 1 out of 2 (or 5 out of 10 or...) he
assigns a likelihood of .5 and, in general, if he thinks the
chances of an event are x out of y, he assigns a likelihood
of x/y. Joe decides to do the same thing in analyzing his ship-
buying problem. On this basis the likelihood of a peach is .8
and the likelihood of a lemon is .2. When likelihoods are expressed in this manner, we will call the likelihoods *probabilities*.* As simply a matter of shorthand, we will denote the
probability of any event, E, by the symbols "Pr(E)." Thus, for
Joe, Pr(P) = .8 and Pr(L) = .2.

> One of the advantages of expressing likelihoods
> as probabilities is that these probabilities can
> be represented as relative areas in a simple graphic
> device known as a Venn diagram. To see this, we
> will need some definitions describing precisely
> what we mean by an event.

---

*In Chapter 2, we will give a considerably more precise
 definition of what a probability is.

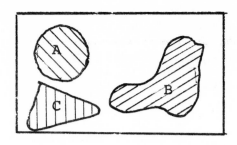

An **event** is a well-defined outcome or set of outcomes of an
experiment. (An *experiment* is
any process whose outcome is
not known with certainty by
the decision-maker.) Events
can be visualized as collections
of points or areas like those
shown in the space at left,
which space represents the
set of all possible outcomes
of the experiment.

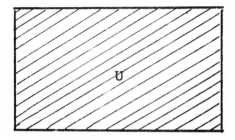

The collection of all possible
outcomes of the experiment is
called U, the **universal event**.
In Joe's case there are only
two possible outcomes. Hence,
U equals the combined event
"Nature comes up with either
a peach or a lemon."

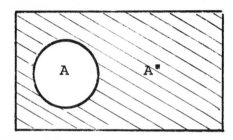

Event A', the *complement* of
event A, is the collection of
all points in the universal
set which are not included in
event A. In Joe's problem the
complement of P is L and the
complement of L is P.

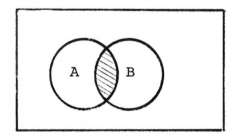

The *intersection* of two events
A and B is the collection of all
outcomes which are contained
both in A and in B. The intersection of A and B is denoted
AB. The intersection of the
only two possible outcomes in
Joe's tree, P and L, contains
no outcomes because P and L
don't overlap, in which case
we say the intersection is
empty.

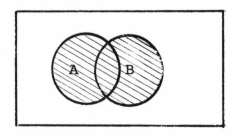

The *union* of two events A and B
is the collection of all outcomes which are either in A or
in B or both. The union of
A and B is denoted A+B. As
noted earlier, in Joe's case
the union of P and L is the
whole space.

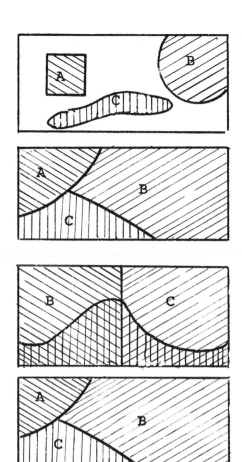

A list of events, $A_1, A_2 \ldots, A_n$ are said to be mutually exclusive if no outcome is contained in more than one member of the list. Both the lists to the left are mutually exclusive. The events P and L in Joe's problem are mutually exclusive.

A list of events, $A_1, A_2 \ldots, A_n$ is said to be *collectively exhaustive* if every outcome is a member of at least one of the events in the list. Both the lists to the left are collectively exhaustive. The events P and L are collectively exhaustive.

We can represent the probability of an event by the amount of space in the Venn diagram which the event takes up. An event is certain to occur only if all possible outcomes of an experiment are included in it. Its probability is 1.00 and it takes up the entire space. If an even is certain to not occur, it takes up no space and, in general, if the probability of an event is .x, then it takes up x% of the space. For Joe's problem the situation can be represented.

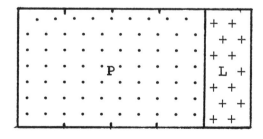

We will use this representation below in helping Joe to think about his problem.

Returning to the decision tree representation of Joe's problem we shall indicate the probability with which Nature makes her choices on branches emanating from chance nodes by writing above the beginning of each such branch the probability that Nature will follow that branch. In the present example, the probability associated with the branch marked P is .8 and that associated with the branch marked L is .2. Joe's decision tree with the probabilities included is shown in Figure 1.2.

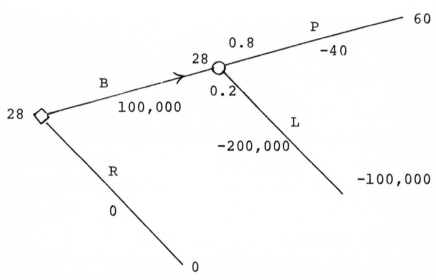

FIGURE 1.2

JOE'S DECISION TREE WITH PROBABILITIES

Figure 1.2 is a complete representation of Joe's problem. Which course of action should Joe choose? Some decision-makers (DMs) will decide on Refuse to Buy right off because they realize that there is at least some chance of losing $100,000 and the potential winnings ($60,000) is not nearly high enough for them to justify the gamble. There is nothing irrational about this. Fairly frequently, for example, a person is not willing to pay even $10 for a fifty-fifty chance at $0 or $100. There are, however, other people who will pay $49 or up to $50 for this same gamble. There are still others who will pay $52 or more because they are willing to pay a premium for the thrill

10

of the game, for "action" or perhaps because they feel that they can't do what they want to do with the $52 they now have, but if they had $100 everything would be ideal. In general, people's attitudes toward the possible consequences can vary over a wide range. It is unreasonable to expect that people will gamble alike.

In this introductory chapter, we will arbitrarily assume that Joe is an EMV'er. EMV'ers constitute the class of people who are willing to make choices under uncertainty on the basis of maximizing *expected monetary value* (EMV). The EMV of a gamble that results in a payoff of $0 or $100 with equal probabilities of 1/2 is:

$$1/2(0)+1/2(100)=\$50$$

In general, one obtains the EMV of a gamble with several possible outcomes by multiplying each cash outcome by its probability and summing these products over all possible outcomes. Thus, if there are N possible outcomes and the nth outcome has a cash value of x_n and the DM thinks its likelihood is p_n, the EMV of this gamble for this DM is

$$p_1x_1+p_2x_2+\dots p_Nx_N = \sum_{n=1}^{N} p_m\ x_m$$

An EMV'er is a person who, when faced with a number of gambles, always desires to choose that gamble with highest EMV.

In Joe's case, there are two possible outcomes resulting from buying the ship (+60,-100) with probabilities (.8,.2) respectively. Hence the EMV associated with purchasing the ship is:

$$.8(60K)+.2(-100K) = 28K$$

If he refuses to buy the ship, then he can assure himself an outcome of 0. That is, with probability 1.0 the result will be zero. Thus, the EMV associated with not buying the ship is:

$$1.0(0K) = 0K$$

11

The EMV'er by definition acts so as to maximize expected monetary value. In this case, the EMV maximizing choice is to buy the ship. The decision consistent with expected monetary value decision-making is indicated by drawing a solid arrowhead on the B branch leading from the decision node. We then write his expected gain from taking that branch above the node associated with the decision.

It is very important to realize that the adjective "expected" in the term expected value does *not* have its everyday meaning. An expected value of +28,000 does not mean that the DM expects to obtain the amount 28,000 dollars. In this case, purchase implies Joe will gain either $60,000 or lose $100,000, neither of which amounts is very close to $28,000. Expected value is merely the average of the dollar outcomes weighted by the likelihood of the outcome.

1.3 THE STRANGER APPEARS

As a result of this analysis of the problem, Joe feels a little better than he did before. He has forsaken all hope of $100K monetary gain and is coming around to the idea that it might be wise to settle for an expected gain of $28K. However, just when he is becoming reconciled to the forces of fate, a stranger approaches him and says, "I couldn't help overhearing you talking to yourself about your problems. Perhaps I can help you. You see I worked in the yard where the substandard ships or lemons as you call them were made. I can tell you whether the ship sitting on this berth is a lemon simply by looking at the serial number." Joe can hardly believe his ears. At last a possibility of finding out whether the ship is a lemon before buying it.

Joe looks at the man, decides he has an honest appearance, and says, "You are just the kind of help I need. Let's go over to the ship and take a look at it. I am eager to find out whether or not it is a good deal." The stranger smiles and replies, "I am sure you are, but you can hardly expect me to go to all the trouble of examining the ship and getting myself

12

dirty without some financial consideration." At first Joe is angry about the stranger's mercenary attitude, but then he remembers he is not in a position to throw away potentially useful information if it can be obtained at a reasonable price. He asks for and is granted a few moments to think over the stranger's offer.

The problem is this: how much is Joe willing to pay the stranger for his information? He reasons as follows. On the basis of the stranger's appearance and manner, Joe decides that he can be trusted in his claim of being able to distinguish peaches from lemons. If the stranger reports that the ship is a peach, then Joe will buy it and make a net gain of $60K. If the stranger says it is a lemon, then Joe will refuse to buy it and make nothing. Joe's probability that the stranger will find a peach is 0.8 and the probability of his finding a lemon is 0.2. Consequently, Joe's expected gain before receiving the information is $0.8(60)+.2(0)=\$48K$. Therefore, is the information worth $48K? No, not to an EMV'er because, even without it, Joe can obtain an EMV of $28K according to our original analysis. Hence, the net value of the stranger's information to Joe is $20K. That is, Joe as an expected-value decision-maker should be willing to pay any amount up to $20K for the stranger's advice.

We shall call this quantity the expected value of perfect information or the EVPI. It represents the maximum price that an EMV'er should pay for experimental results when pricing a decision under uncertainty. This follows since no partial knowledge could ever be worth more than a report of the actual outcome of Nature's process.

1.4 THE GUARANTEE

Joe now decides to offer the stranger $15K in hopes of getting the information at a bargain price. However, when he confronts the stranger with this offer, the stranger replies that he couldn't consider the job for less than $25,000 and

13

suggests that Joe think it over for a while. Joe is upset by this turn of events, but quickly regains his composure. He thinks to himself that the real reason for his difficulties is that he doesn't have a wide enough range of alternatives from which to select an appropriate action. Suddenly he has a brain-storm--maybe he can get the broker to give him a guarantee on the ship! He inquires of the broker whether he would be willing to underwrite the ship's repair bills. The broker says, "Yes, there is a guarantee plan, it costs $60,000 and covers 50% of repair cost." Joe thinks fast and replies, "You certainly don't have much confidence in this ship. If I bought the ship and it turned out to be a lemon, I could go broke even on my 50%." The broker says, "All right, just for you I will include an anti-lemon feature in the guarantee. If total repairs on the ship cost you $100,000 or more, I will pay for *any* of the repairs. How is that for meeting a customer halfway?" Joe says, "That's fine, and now I would like to think things over again."

At this point Joe realizes that he has a new decision tree. It is shown in Figure 1.3. This tree differs from the preceding one because there are now three possible actions at the decision node. The new alternative is to buy the ship with the guarantee; that is, to hedge against the possibility of getting a lemon by spending $60,000. This alternative is given the symbol G. We see that, although the ship might still turn out to be a lemon if this alternative is followed, the costs associated with the two outcomes are strikingly different from what they are in the case where the ship is bought without such a guarantee.

Let us examine Figure 1.3 in some detail. The figures written below each branch are again the gain or loss associated with traversing that branch. The numbers on the tips are the total expected monetary value of the chain of branches leading to that tip.

The expected value of the nodes B and R are calculated as before. The value of $40K written under the G branch refers to

14

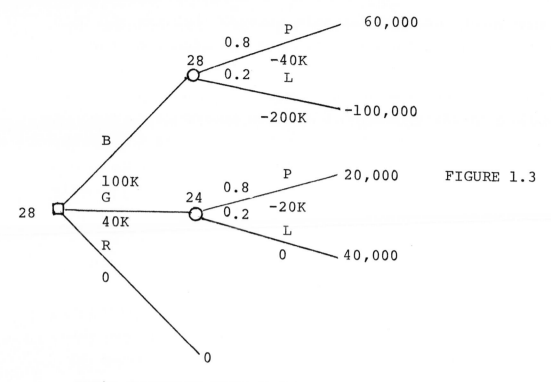

FIGURE 1.3

JOE'S DECISION TREE INCLUDING GUARANTEE POSSIBILITY

the fact that our initial gain from buying the ship with the guarantee is only $40K because the guarantee itself costs $60K. The value of -$20K over the P branch following the G action arises because even a peach will require one repair at a cost of $40K, but half of this $40K will be paid by the guarantee. The 0 under the corresponding L branch is a result of the anti-lemon feature of the guarantee. Since the cost of repairs on a lemon will exceed $100K, there will be no charge for repairs. Thus, the gain associated with buying the ship with a guarantee and having it turn out to be a peach is $20K, while the gain if it turns out to be a lemon is $40K. The probabilities of these two events have values of 0.8 and 0.2 respectively. Hence, the EMV from buying the ship with the guarantee is 0.8(20)+0.2(40) = $24,000. Since this is less than the $28K EMV associated with buying the ship without the guarantee, buying the guarantee is not consistent with the objective we have assumed for Joe: maximum expected monetary value. Under this objective, the choice should once more be to buy the ship without any protection, as is indicated by the heavy arrowhead on the B branch.

15

At this point our knowledgeable stranger returns and once more offers his advice-for-a-price. Has the advent of the guarantee changed what Joe should pay? Let's find out. If the information is bought, the stranger will find that the ship is a peach with probability 0.8. If a peach is reported, then Joe will buy it without a guarantee and obtain a net gain of $60K. With probability 0.2 the stranger will discover a lemon. In this case, however, Joe is best advised not to refuse the ship and make nothing as he did before, but rather to buy it with the guarantee. As the number on the tip of the branch GL in Figure 1.3 indicates, by taking this action he will obtain a net gain of $40K. Thus, the EMV associated with buying the ship with the stranger's information is 0.8(60)+0.2(40)=$56K. Since Joe can obtain an EMV of $28K anyway by buying the ship without this information, the net value of the additional information to him is $28K.

It may at first seem strange that the expected value of perfect information, or EVPI, should increase simply because an alternative has been added to those already available to Joe. However, such an increase has taken place as a result of the fact that Joe is in a better position to make use of information that the ship is a lemon than he was previously. Now the stranger's asking price of $25K for the perfect information seems quite reasonable. Joe is about to purchase the information when he has another brainstorm. He knows that perfect information is worth $28,000 to him, and so he reasons that if he can get partial information at a price sufficiently lower than $28,000 he may be able to increase his EMV.

1.5 THE YARD'S TEST PLANS

Joe calls a friend at a nearby yard to ask what kind of tests could be performed and how much they would cost. The yardman says he is very busy and that he can only do at the most one or two tests on the ship in the time available. He then supplies Joe with the following test alternatives:

1. He can test the steering system alone at a cost of $9,000;
2. He can test two systems—the fuel and electrical systems—for a total cost of $13,000;
3. He can perform a two-test sequence in which Joe will be able to authorize the second test after the result of the first test is known. Under this alternative, the yard will test the turbine at a cost of $10,000, report the outcome of the test to Joe, and then proceed to check the reduction gears at an additional cost of $4,000, if it is requested to do so.

All the tests will find a defect in each system tested if a defect exists. The test alternatives are summarized in Table 1.1 including the possibility of no testing.

Joe looks over these test alternatives and decides that it is worthwhile to at least consider testing because the cost of each of these tests is significantly less than the $28,000 expected value of perfect information. If all tests had cost over $28K, then there would be no point in considering a testing program because each test will generally provide only partial information, and even perfect information is worth a maximum of $28K. However, it is still not clear which test, if any, should be performed. Furthermore, Joe would like to know the

TABLE 1.1

THE TEST ALTERNATIVES

Test	Description	Cost
T_0	Perform no test	$0
T_1	Test steering system	9,000
T_2	Test fuel and electrical systems (2 systems)	13,000
T_3	Test turbine with option on testing gear	10,000 (optional) + 4,000

value of the stranger's information under these new circumstances. These problems will be approached by drawing a new decision tree for Joe. The general structure of the decision tree is shown in Figure 1.4.

The tree is a little complicated, so we shall explain it in steps. Notice that the first decision to be made is which of the four test options--T_0, T_1, T_2, T_3--to follow. If some tests are made, the yard will report the results, and then a decision about buying the ship must be made. If the test T_3 is used, then there will also be a step in which the yard is advised whether or not to continue the test procedure. Let us now examine the situation resulting from each test in more detail.

If test T_0 is selected, then no physical test is made and Joe is required to make a decision about buying the ship immediately. The decision tree from this point on looks just like that of Figure 1.3. In fact, the numbers that appear in Figure 1.3 have been reproduced exactly in Figure 1.4 with the exception that only the numbers on the tips of the branches have been copied because they are sufficient for our purposes. Indeed, a little reflection will reveal that, regardless of the test program we follow, we must end up with a decision tree like that of Figure 1.3. However, although the numbers on the tips of the branches will be the same in all cases, the probabilities to be written on the branches will differ in each case. The probability of the final outcome of a peach or a lemon will generally depend on the findings of the experimental program up to the time the decision on buying the ship must be made. For example, if two defects have been found, then Joe can be absolutely sure that the ship is a lemon.

We see that what is now required is a mechanism that will give for each possible result of the experimental program the appropriate probabilities for the ultimate outcome of a peach and a lemon.

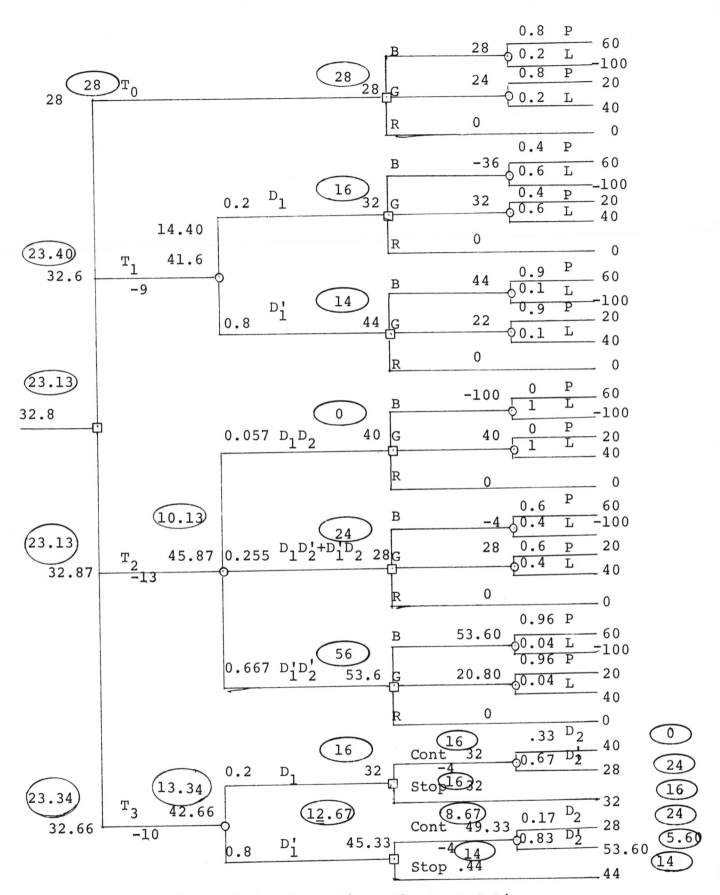

Joe's Decision Tree Given the Test Options
(All monetary figures in thousands of dollars.)

FIGURE 1.4
19

To develop such a mechanism, let us concentrate on that part of the tree associated with test plan T_1 which we have reproduced below. For now, ignore the probabilities which have been assigned to various chance events in this tree.

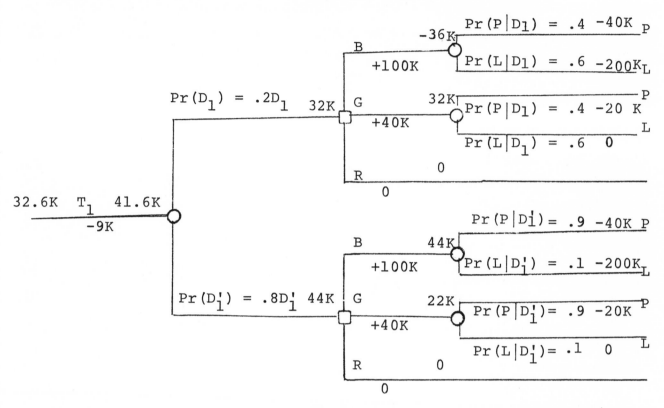

FIGURE 1-5

D_1 denotes the event "a defect is discovered on the first (in this case, the only) test" and D_1' denotes the complementary event "no defect discovered on the first test." Thus, this portion of the tree indicates that, if Joe decides on T_1, he will pay out $9,000, then Nature will determine either D_1 or D_1', after which Joe will be faced with the Buy, Guarantee, or Refuse option, and finally Nature will choose either a peach or a lemon. Since we already know the rewards associated with each branch, this subtree is complete except for the probabilities to be assigned to the branches emanating from the chance nodes.

In the case of the no-test option the assignments were obvious. If Joe believed the broker knew what he was talking about, then $Pr(P) = .8$ and $Pr(L) = .2$. Now things are a little

20

more complicated. Suppose Joe chooses T_1 and the test reveals a defect, i.e., Joe is at node D_1 on the subtree. Presumably, the information he has obtained, if it is worth anything at all, should increase his likelihood that the ship is a lemon and decrease the likelihood that the ship is a peach. The question is: by how much should these probabilities change? Further, in order to compare test option T_1 with the other possible tests, we will need to assign probabilities to the branches emanating from node T_1. In short, in order to evaluate this subtree, we need to know the following six quantities:

a) The likelihood of a peach given that the test has revealed a defect, denoted $Pr(P|D_1)$ and read "the conditional probability of event P given that event D_1 has occurred" or usually "the conditional probability of P given D_1,"

b) The conditional probability of a lemon given that the test revealed a defect, or $Pr(L|D_1)$,

c) The conditional probability of a peach given that the test revealed no defect, or $Pr(P|D_1')$,

d) The conditional probability of a lemon given that the test revealed no defect, or $Pr(L|D_1')$,

e) The probability that test option T_1 will discover a defect or $Pr(D_1)$,

f) That probability that test option T_1 will reveal no defect on $Pr(D_1')$.

What information does Joe have which might enable him to compute these probabilities? Well, he already knows the following six probabilities:

1. Joe's probability the ship is a peach before any testing, $Pr(P)=.8$.

2. The probability the ship is a lemon before any testing, $Pr(L)=.2$.

3. The conditional probability that the test will reveal a defect if the ship is a peach, $Pr(D_1|P)=.1*$.

---

*We are tacitly assuming that the ship's defects are equally likely to occur in each of the ten systems.

21

4. The conditional probability that the test will not reveal a defect if the ship is a peach, $Pr(D_1'|P)=.9$.
5. The conditional probability that the test will reveal a defect if the ship is a lemon, $Pr(D_1|L)=.6$.
6. The conditional probability that the test will not reveal a defect if the ship is a lemon, $Pr(D_1'|L)=.4$.

How can we use these probabilities to obtain the probabilities that Joe needs? Let's start with the probability of a defect, $Pr(D_1)$. Joe realizes there are two mutually exclusive ways he can get a defect. Either the ship is a peach and the test happens to hit on the single defective system which occurrence is represented by the compound event PD_1 (remember this is read 'P and D_1') or the ship is a lemon and we happen to test one of the six defective systems which is the event LD_1. In other words, a long-winded way of saying the event D_1 is PD_1+LD_1 (read 'P and D_1 or L and D_1'). The situation is represented by the following diagram.

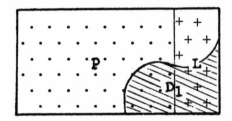

Now Joe doesn't know what the probability of the event D_1 is but he does have some ideas concerning the probability of the events PD_1 (the area that is both cross hatched and dotted in the diagram) and LD_1 (the area that is both cross hatched and crossed in the diagram). He reasons "the probability of a peach is .8. If the ship is a peach, the chances of a defect are 1 in 10 (or, more concisely, $Pr(D_1|P)=.1$). Hence, to get both a peach and a defect, I have to survive, first, a .8 gamble and then a .1 gamble. My chances of doing that are .8 x .1 or .08. The probability of PD_1 is .08."

Joe has deduced that the following relations hold between

22

the various events P, D_1 and PD_1:

$$Pr(PD_1) = Pr(P)Pr(D_1|P)$$

We shall call this the Product Rule. It says the probability of the intersection of any two events is equal to the probability of one of the events times the conditional probability of the other event given the first. By similar reasoning

$$Pr(LD_1) = Pr(L)Pr(D_1|L)$$

$$= .2 \cdot .6 = .12.$$

Of course, Joe is not directly interested in $Pr(PD_1)$ or $Pr(LD_1)$ but rather the probability of simply D_1, $Pr(D_1)$. However, Joe has noticed from his horse-racing days that one of the nice things about expressing likelihoods in the form of probabilities is that if one has two events, for example, the event A might be "the #3 horse wins a certain race" and the event B might be "the #4 horse wins this race," which cannot both occur simultaneously, then the probability of the compound event "either A or B or both happen" which we have denoted A+B (read 'A or B') is equal to the sum of the probabilities of the individual events. Joe realizes that in running probabilities in this manner he must be careful to deal only with events which cannot both occur, events which in our terms are mutually exclusive. For example, he knows that the fact that his probability of the event C, "the #3 horse places (finishes second or better)" is .5 and his probability of the event D, "the #4 horse places" is also .5, does *not* mean that his probability of the event "either the #3 or the #4 horse places" is 1.0. In this case, the two events C and D are not mutually exclusive, in which case the probabilities will not add.

Joe realizes he had better stop ruminating on his misspent days at the horse track and get on with his problem. He needs $Pr(D_1)$ and he has $Pr(PD_1)$ and $Pr(LD_1)$. But the events PD_1 and LD_1 are mutually exclusive, since the first requires that the ship be a peach and the second requires that the ship be a lemon. Hence,

$$Pr(PD_1 + LD_1) = Pr(PD_1) + Pr(LD_1)$$

but "ship is a peach and system tested is defective or ship is a lemon and system tested is defective" is just a long-winded way of saying "system tested is defective." That is, the event $PD_1 + LD_1$ equals the event D_1. This is obvious from the diagram on page 1-23. In summary,

$$Pr(D_1) = Pr(PD_1) + Pr(LD_1)$$

We can put this expression in terms of the probabilities that Joe was originally given by substituting the Product Rule into both probabilities on the right-hand side.

$$Pr(D_1) = Pr(D_1|P)Pr(P) + Pr(D_1|L)Pr(L)$$
$$= (.1) \cdot (.8) + (.6) \cdot (.2) = .2$$

We shall have occasion to use this simple result, which we will call the Sum Rule, many times in what follows.

By a similar argument, the probability of the event "no defect on first system tested," D_1', is

$$Pr(D_1') = Pr(D_1'|P)Pr(P) + Pr(D_1'|L)Pr(L)$$
$$= (.9) \cdot (.8) + (.4) \cdot (.2) = .8$$

Of course, since $D_1 + D_1' = U$ and D_1 and D_1' are mutually exclusive, we could have obtained the probability of D_1' directly from

$$Pr(D_1') = 1.0 - Pr(D_1)$$

with the same result.

Well, Joe now has $Pr(D_1)$ and $Prr(D_1')$ and he enters them into the proper places on Figure 1.5. He still needs $Pr(P|D_1)$, $Pr(L|D_1)$, $Pr(P|D_1')$ and $Pr(L|D_1')$. Let us work on $Pr(P|D_1)$. Examining his Venn diagram,

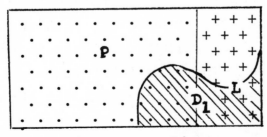

24

Joe says to himself. "Having observed a defect, I am certain that D_1 has occurred. My new probability on the event D_1 is 1.0 and the new probability on D_1' is 0.0. It is as if D_1 becomes the new universal event and I throw away everything outside D_1. I have no information which would lead me to alter the relative probabilities of the events within D_1. Therefore, in order to get my new probability on P, all I need to know is what percentage of D_1 is taken up by P. Well, that is simple; the total area of D_1 is .2 of which .08 is in P since $D_2 P$ = .08. Hence, in the new space, i.e., given D_1, the relative area of P is .08/.2 = .4. My chances of getting a peach after having observed a defect, $\Pr(P|D_1)$, equals .4. Eureka."

Joe is justifiably proud of himself, but all that he has really done is to rediscover the Product Rule. He has reasoned that
$$\Pr(P|D_1) = \Pr(PD_1)/\Pr(D_1)$$
which is just a slightly altered form of the Product Rule. By substituting the Product Rule and the Sum Rule into the righthand side of this expression, we obtain

$$\Pr(P|D_1) = \frac{\Pr(D_1|P)\Pr(P)}{\Pr(D_1|P)\Pr(P) + \Pr(D_1|L)\Pr(L)}$$

which is known as Bayes Rule. The significance of Bayes Rule is that it allows the decision-maker to flip the events in conditional probabilities which is just what he needs if he is to interpret correctly the effect of less than perfect information. The reason is that the DM usually knows the probability of each experimental result as a function of the underlying state of Nature, that is, probabilities such as $P(D_1|P)$. But what he needs to know to evaluate his tree are the probabilities of the underlying state of Nature as a function of the experimental results, probabilities such as $\Pr(P|D_1)$. Joe is beside himself. By similar reasoning he quickly finds

$$\Pr(L|D_1) = \frac{\Pr(D_1|L)\Pr(L)}{\Pr(D_1)} = \frac{(.6)\cdot(.2)}{(.2)} = .6$$

$$\Pr(P|D_1') = \frac{\Pr(D_1'|P)\Pr(P)}{\Pr(D_1')} = \frac{(.9)\cdot(.8)}{(.8)} = .9$$

$$Pr(L|D_1') = \frac{Pr(D_1'|L)Pr(L)}{Pr(D_1')} = \frac{(.4) \cdot (.2)}{(.8)} = .1$$

Notice the $Pr(P|D_1)$ and $Pr(L|D_1)$ sum to 1.00, as they must for after we have observed a defect the ship must still be either a peach or a lemon. Similarly for $Pr(P|D_1')$ and $Pr(L|D_1')$. Notice also that this test will change Joe's feelings about his chances quite significantly. If it reveals a defect, the probability of a lemon jumps from .2 to .6. If it reveals no defect, the probability of a lemon drops to .1.

We now have all the probabilities we need for assignment to the subtree associated with test option T_1. We have made these assignments in Figure 1.5. Notice that the sum of the probabilities on the branches emanating from any chance node is 1.0, as they must, for we constructed the tree in such a way that at any chance node, Nature must choose exactly one of the branches.

Having assigned these probabilities we are in a position to begin folding back the subtree of Figure 1.5. Let's start with the upper right-hand corner of the subtree. Here, Joe buys the ship without a guarantee after observing a defect in the system tested. His probability of a peach is .4 and of a lemon is .6. Hence, the EMV associated with this experimental outcome and decision is $(.4)(60K)+.6(-100K)=-36K$. We have assigned this value to the corresponding node in Figure 1.5. If Joe buys with with a guarantee after observing a defect, the same probabilities will apply but now the monetary outcomes are 20K and 40K respectively. Thus, the EMV of this choice is +32K. As before, the EMV of the refusal option is 0. We are now in a position to evaluate the decision at node D_1. Clearly, the EMV maximizing option, having observed a defect on a single test, is to buy with guarantee, which option has a value of 32K. We have associated this value with node D_1.

We can handle the D_1' branch of T_1 similarly, only now the probability of a peach is .9 and that of a lemon is .1. Hence, having observed no defect on the system tested the EMV of buying the ship with guarantee is $(.9)(20K+(.1)(40K)=22K$, and the EMV of refusal is still 0. If Joe does not observe a defect on the system tested, he will maximize his EMV by buying the ship without a guarantee and the value of this decision has been associated with its node.

There is but one step remaining in the analysis of test option T_1. If the yard reports a defect, Joe expects to gain $32,000. If it reports no defect, then Joe expects to gain $44K. These two events happen with probability 0.2 and 0.8, respectively, according to the earlier calculations. Hence, the expected net gain before the results of the test are known, but after the test has been paid for, is 0.2(32)+0.8(44)=$41,600. Since Joe must pay the yard $9,000 to reach this position, his expected earnings from test T_1, including the payment to the yard are $41,600-$9,000=$32,600. This number is entered at the left of branch T_1 to indicate the expected gain from following this test program. Since we have already calculated the EMV of program T_0 to be $28,000, it is clear that Joe will increase his EMV by proceeding with the test on the steering rather than by making the purchase decision in the absence of this information. By so doing he will increase his expected gain by $4,600. Of course, it is still not proven that T_1 is the best test alternative for an EMV'er to follow--we have only shown that it is better than T_0. It remains to investigate T_2 and T_3.

Before we do so, however, let us return once more to the concept of the value of perfect information. We have already shown that the partial information supplied by option T_1 is more valuable than its cost. How has this revelation affected our evaluation of the stranger's information? Before the test alternatives were introduced, Joe had calculated that the expected value of perfect information was $28,000. As you recall, this figure was determined by calculating first the amount of money Joe could make if the perfect information was available to him ($56,000) and then subtracting from this quantity the amount he could expect to earn in the absence of this information ($28,000); thus, EVPI equaled $56,000-$28,000. Now what has changed in these calculations? $56,000, the EMV associated with perfect information has remained unchanged since the introduction of the guarantee plan. However, Joe's expectation without the stranger's information has been increased from \$28,000 to \$33,600. Hence, the expected value of perfect information has been lowered to \$56,000-\$32,400 = \$23,400.

The value of perfect information at each point in the tree is shown in Figure 1.4 in the ovals at pertinent nodes. *In every case the EVPI is calculated simply by subtracting the expected earnings at each node from Joe's EMV just before obtaining the perfect information.* At the two nodes that begin and end branch T_1 the result of the test is not known and so the expected gain using perfect information is still \$56,000. Thus, the node to the right of branch T_1 bears the EVPI \$14,000 since \$56,000-\$41,600=\$14,400. Perfect information is worth \$9,000 less than it was to the right of branch T_1 because the payment to the yard is no longer variable. It is a sunk cost.

The calculation of the value of perfect information is performed in the same way when the test results are known, but, in this case, the expected gain from using the perfect information is different. Consider the situation where a defect has been reported. Joe knows that if the ship is a peach he should buy it without the guarantee and make \$60,000 and that if it is a lemon he should buy it with a guarantee and make \$40,000. Now that a defect has been reported, the probabilities of a peach and a lemon have changed to 0.4 and 0.6 respectively. Thus, the expected gain using perfect information is now 0.4(60K)+0.6(40K)=\$48,000. It is from this quantity that the expected value of node T_1D_1, \$32,000 must be subtracted in order to obtain the EVPI of \$16,000 entered in the oval above node T_1D_1.

Similarly, we see that if no defect had been reported, the probabilities of peach and lemon would be 0.9 and 0.1, and the expected gain of using perfect information would be 0.9(60)+ 0.1(40)=\$58,000. When we subtract the \$44K value of node T_1D_1', we obtain the $14,000 figure for the EVPI that is pertinent to that node.

Let us now move forward to an analysis of test option T_2. In this case, as you will recall, two systems on the ship--the fuel and electrical systems--are subjected to test and then the results of both tests are reported to Joe. The possible reports are that 2, 1, or 0 defects were found. These three events are represented by the three branches D_1D_2, $D_1D_2'+D_1'D_2$ and $D_1'D_2'$ that are drawn to the right of node T_3 in the tree of Figure 1.4. When the yard's report is known, Joe must make a decision on buying the ship, using a decision tree similar to that shown in Figure 1.3. The expected earnings at the tips of the tree remain the same, but once more we require a new assignment of the ultimate probabilities of a peach and a lemon as a result of the shipyard's report. The probabilities necessary are: $Pr(D_1D_2)$, $Pr(D_1D_2'+D_1'D_2)$, $Pr(D_1'D_2')$, $Pr(P|D_1D_2)$, $Pr(L|D_1D_2)$, $Pr(P|D_1D_2'+D_1'D_2)$, $Pr(L|D_1D_2'+D_1'D_2)$, $Pr(P|D_1'D_2')$ and $Pr(L|D_1'D_2')$.

We could obtain these probabilities from the probabilities we already know by proper application of the Product Rule and the Sum Rule as we did to T_1. However, since the number of probabilities involved is beginning to mount up, it may pay us to be a little more systematic in keeping track of these various probabilities. As a device for structuring our probabilistic calculations, let us introduce Nature's tree.

We have seen that Bayes Rule is a method for flipping the events in conditional probabilities. In a similar vein, we might flip the order in which Nature makes her choices at chance nodes. For example, in the problem at hand, we might regard Nature as choosing either a peach or a lemon and then making her choices with respect to the test results. A tree describing this sequence of moves is shown in Figure 1.6. We shall call such a flipped tree, Nature's tree.

All nodes in Nature's tree are chance nodes. In the problem at hand, the tree consists of three tiers of branches. The first node represents Nature's choice of a peach or a lemon, the second set of nodes represents Nature's choice of a defect or not on the first system tested and the third set of nodes represents Nature's choice of a defect or not on the second system tested. When Nature's choices are arranged in this order it is an easy matter to assign probabilities to the various branches in Figure 1.6.

The unconditional probability of Nature's choosing a peach is .8 and a lemon is .2. These probabilities have been assigned to the branches emanating from the leftmost node. Suppose the ship has turned out to be a peach. Then, we are at node P. Now suppose that one major system of the ship is tested. Since the ship is a peach, there is probability 1 in 10, or 0.1 that the one defective system will be checked and found defective; thus, $Pr(D_1|P)=.1$. By the Product Rule, the probability of both P and D_1, the probability of getting to node PD_1 is $PR(PD_1)=Pr(P)\cdot Pr(D_1|P)=0.08$. In other words, the Product Rule says that the probability of getting to a node is the product of the branch probabilities leading to that node. Suppose that a second test on another system is now performed. If we are at node PD_1, then the only defective system in the ship has already been discovered and there is probability 0 of finding another defect and reaching node PD_1D_2. Under these circumstances, we shall be certain to proceed to node PD_1D_2'. By applying the Product Rule twice, the probability of the event PD_1D_2 is deter-mined by multiplying together the probabilities on all the branches that lead to that tip of the tree. Thus, $Pr(PD_1D_2)=Pr(D_2|D_1P)\cdot Pr(D_1|P)\cdot Pr(P)$ and $Pr(PD_1D_2')=Pr(D_2'|D_1P)\cdot Pr(D_1|P)\cdot Pr(P)$.

If the ship were a peach, but no defect had been found on the first test, then we would be at node PD_1'. If now a second test is performed, it will yield a defect with the probability that the system tested is the one defective system in the remaining nine or 1/9. Of course, the probability of finding no

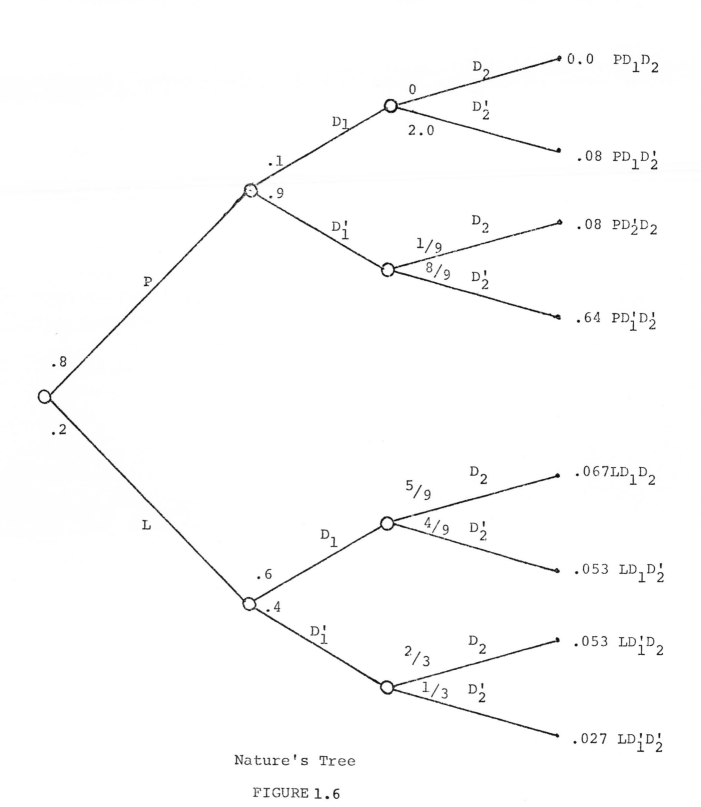

Nature's Tree

FIGURE 1.6

31

defect in this situation is then 8/9. The probabilities $P(PD_1'D_2)=$ 0.08 and $P(PD_1'D_2')= 0.64$ can then be calculated by multiplying the relevant branch probabilities.

If Nature selects a lemon initially, then the same sort of reasoning applies. The probability of finding a defect in the first test on a lemon is equal to the chance of testing one of the six defective systems out of the 10 systems on the ship, or 0.6. If one defect has been found in a lemon, then the probability of finding another is the chance that one of the 5 defective systems among the remaining 9 systems will be inspected, or 5/9. If, on the other hand, no defect is found in the first test on a lemon, then the probability of finding one during the second test is the chance of testing one of the 6 defective systems among the 9 systems remaining, or 2/3. The probabilities of all final outcomes pertaining to the lemon branch of the tree are then computed and written on the tips of the branches. Figure 1.6 contains all the information necessary to answer any question about the probabilistic structure of the decision process.

We can best see this by returning at this point to our discussion of the test alternative T_2 in Figure 1.4. For example, the probabilities $Pr(D_1D_2)$, $Pr(D_1D_2'+D_1'D_2)$ and $Pr(D_1'D_2')$ can be obtained by simply adding the tip probabilities in Figure 1.6 which correspond to the desired event, i.e., by using the Sum Rule. For example, the event D_1D_2 is the same as the event 'D_1D_2 and a peach or D_1D_2 and a lemon'. The probabilities corresponding to the latter two events are $Pr(D_1D_2P)=0$ and $Pr(D_1D_2L)=.067$. In short, by the Sum Rule

$$Pr(D_1D_2)=Pr(D_1D_2P)+Pr(D_1D_2L)=0+.067=.067 \quad .$$

Similarly,

$$Pr(D_1D_2'+D_1'D_2)=Pr(D_1D_2'P)+Pr(D_1D_2'L)+Pr(D_1'D_2P)+Pr(D_1'D_2L)$$

$$=.08+.053+.08+.053=.266$$

and

$$Pr(D_1'D_2')=Pr(D_1'D_2'P)+Pr(D_1'D_2'L)=.64+.027=.677 \quad .$$

With these probabilities and the tip probabilities, it is a simple matter to obtain the desired conditional probabilities by solving for the conditional probability in the Product Rule. For example,

$$\Pr(P|D_1'D_2') = \Pr(D_1'D_2'P)/\Pr(D_1'D_2')$$

$$= .64/.667 = .96$$

The probability of a lemon given $D_1 D_2$ is equal to 1.0 minus this probability or $\Pr(L|D_1'D_2') = .04$. Similarly,

$$\Pr(P|D_1 D_2) = \Pr(D_1 D_2 P)/\Pr(D_1 D_2) = 0/.067 = 0$$

$$\Pr(P|D_1 D_2' + D_1' D_2) = \frac{\Pr(PD_1 D_2') + \Pr(PD_1' D_1)}{\Pr(D_1 D_2' + D_1' D_2)}$$

$$= \frac{.08 + .08}{.266} = .6$$

And, hence, $\Pr(L|D_1 D_2) = 1.0 - 0. = 1.0$ and $\Pr(L|D_1 D_2' + D_1' D_2) = 1.0 - .6 = .4$.

Thus, we see that after Joe has committed himself to test plan T_2, the probabilities that the yard will report 2, 1, or 0 defects are .067, .266, and .667 respectively. These numbers have been entered in Figure 1.4 on the three branches leaving chance node T_2. If two defects are reported, $\Pr(P|D_1 D_2)$ shows that Joe will make his decision with the satisfying but disappointing knowledge that the ship is certain to be a lemon. This information is indicated on the tree by the 0 and 1 entered on the branches P and L that originate in chance nodes $T_1 D_1 D_2 B$, $T_2 D_1 D_2 G$, and $T_3 D_1 D_2 R$. The EMV associated with each of the decisions B, G, and R are -100,000, 40,000 and 0. Consequently, Joe will maximize his EMV by buying the ship with the guarantee, even though it is a lemon, and thus gain $40K. This preferred decision is shown by the solid arrowhead on the branch G following node $T_2 D_1 D_2$; the gain of $40,000 is recorded above that node.

The situation when only one defect is reported is very similar. In this case, we observe from $\Pr(P|D_1 D_2' + D_1' D_2)$ that the probabilities of a peach and a lemon are 0.6 and 0.4. These probabilities appear on the P and L branches at the ends of the sub-tree that follows node $T_2(D_1D_2'+D_1'D_2)$. The EMV of the three actions B, G, and R are $0.6(60)+0.4(-100)=\$4,000; 0.6(20)+0.4(40)=\$28,000$ and \$0. Once more, the highest EMV will result if Joe buys the ship with the guarantee. Note that he does this even though the ship is more likely to be a peach than a lemon. Again we record the expected gain of \$28,000 over the decision node and indicate the preferred decision with a solid arrowhead.

If no defects are reported, the ship is almost certain to be a peach; there is only a four percent chance of its being a lemon. When we compute the expected gain of the three decisions following node $T_3D_1'D_2'$, using the probability 0.96 for a peach and 0.04 for a lemon, we find that buying the ship without a guarantee has an EMV of \$53,000, buying it with a guarantee has an EMV of \$20,000, and not buying it at all has an EMV of 0. Thus, Joe will maximize his EMV by buying the ship without the guarantee, as represented by the solid arrowhead on the B branch following node $T_2D_1'D_2'$ and by the \$53,600 entered over that node.

We have now calculated the EMV maximizing decision and the associated expected earnings for each possible shipyard report under test plan T_3. As we know, chance determines the actual reporting, but we also have learned the probabilities of the yard's reporting 2, 1, or 0 defects, and have entered them in the decision tree. The expected gain to Joe when he is waiting to learn the test results is thus $0.067(40K)+0.226(28K)+0.667(53,600)$ or \$45,870. Of course, in order to reach a situation with this expected value, Joe had to pay out \$13,000.

We might at this point examine once again the expected value of the perfect information offered by the stranger. As we found earlier, this quantity can be calculated at each node of the decision tree simply by subtracting from the expected earnings with perfect information the expected earnings which we have assigned to that node. Accordingly, since the expected gain using perfect information is still \$56K before the test results are known, the value of perfect information when Joe has decided to use test T_2 is $23,130 (i.e., $56,000-$32,870) before he has paid the yard, and $10,130 (i.e., $56,000-$45,870) after the yard has received its $13,000.

However, after the test results have been reported, the expected gain using perfect information is different from $56,000. Remember that Joe can make a profit of $60K if he knows the ship is a peach, and of $40K if he knows it is a lemon. From our tree we see that the pair (Pr(P), Pr(L)) takes on the values (0,1), (0.6,0.4) and (0.96,0.04) according to whether 2, 1, or 0 defects were discovered. Joe's expected gain using perfect information is thus $40,000, $53,000, or $59,200, depending on the defect situation. Since we have already calculated the expected values of these states to be $40,000, $28,000, and $53,600 without perfect information, the EVPI's for them must be $0, $24,000, and $5,600 respectively.

An observation of particular importance may be based on these numbers: although we would expect the amount Joe would be willing to pay the stranger for his perfect information to decrease after he is committed to a test plan, it is not necessary for this situation to obtain for any experimental outcome, but only on the average. Thus, after Joe has decided to follow test plan T_2, he established that the EVPI to him at that point is only $23,130. However, if the yard should report that he had found exactly one defect in the ship, Joe now notices that the EVPI has increased to $24,000, a net gain of $870. This means that, if Joe had decided on T_2 and the stranger's price for his information was $23,500, Joe would refuse the information and go ahead with the test, but then willingly pay $24,000 for the same information if the yard reports only one defect.

The result is really not too surprising when we realize that Joe had already considered the chance of being placed in a situation where the expected value of perfect information is $24,000 when he made his decision at node T_2. When Joe contracted for test plan T_2, he had to consider how every possible outcome of the test--2, 1, or 0 defects--would affect his state of knowledge about the type of ship in the yard. If no defects were found, then Joe would be very confident that the ship is a peach and would be willing to pay only $5,600 to remove his remaining uncertainty. If two defects were found, then the ship is surely a lemon and the stranger cannot tell Joe anything of the value. However, if the yard reports one defect, then Joe does not expect to make any more money from this point into the future than he would have made if no tests whatever had been performed--$28,000. It is important to note that the value of perfect information is $24,000 in this situation rather than the $28,000 figure applicable in the absence of tests. This difference is, of course, due to the fact that the probability that the stranger will discover that the ship is a peach has fallen from 0.8 to 0.6. In short, although the expected value of perfect information cannot increase on an average value basis in such trees, it is possible for it to increase for some of the chance outcomes.

Now let us turn to the evaluation of test plan T_3. Under this option the turbine is tested for $10,000; when the outcome of this test is reported, it is possible to have the yard test the reduction gear for an additional cost of $4,000. Such a test procedure is representative of a large class of experimental plans called sequential tests. Such processes are characterized by the option to decide whether or not to continue testing after the results of the initial tests are known.

The decision tree pertinent to T_3 is shown in Figure 1.4. The development of this tree is once more most easily understood by considering the chronological sequence of the decisions that must be made and their outcomes. The payment of $10,000 to initiate this test plan is indicated by a -10K under the branch T_3. The next event that will occur is the report of the yardman about whether he found a defect in the turbine. Thus, we establish a chance point that generates branches D_1 and D_1'.

Regardless of whether or not a defect has been found, Joe must make a decision on the continuation of the test. His two possible actions--continue on to test the reduction gear and stop testing--are shown by the two branches named CONTINUE and STOP that leave decision nodes T_3D_1 and T_3D_1'. Both of the CONTINUE branches are labeled -4000 to indicate the cost of requesting the testing of the reduction gears.

If Joe decides to stop the testing program after hearing the report on the turbine, he will have to make his final decision on buying the ship having only the information that either a defect was or was not found. But these two situations were also encountered under test plan T_1 after the yardman had made his report. Since Joe finds himself in the same position, they must have the same value to him. (Remember that the money paid out for the performance of the test is a sunk cost at this point and so does not affect the *future* expected earnings.) Consequently, we can immediately enter in the tree at the tips of the T_3D_1 STOP and T_3D_1' STOP branches the same values to be found at nodes T_1T_1 and T_1D_1', $32,000 and $44,000 respectively.

The situation if Joe decides to continue testing after hearing the yard's report on its first test is analogous but not identical. If the CONTINUE option is followed, the next event to take place is the report by the yard on whether it found a defect on the second test. Thus, we create chance points at the T_3D_1 CONTINUE and T_3D_1' CONTINUE nodes and D_2 and D_2' branches emanating from them. However, when we receive the second report from the yard, our total information is that in two tests 2, 1, or 0 defects have been found in the ship. Thus, we are in the same state as we were under test option T_2 after the yard's report was known. The appropriate value of $(T_4D_1$ CONTINUE $D_2)$ is, therefore, the value of $(T_3D_1D_2)$ or 40K; for T_3D_1 CONTINUE D_2' and T_3D_1' CONTINUE D_2 is 28K; and for T_3D_1' CONTINUE D_2' it is $53,600. These numbers have been placed at the pertinent tips of the T_3 test plan tree.

We have been able to evaluate the terminal points of T_3

tree by identifying them with nodes that have been considered earlier. It remains to place the relevant probabilities on the chance nodes in this tree so that we can proceed to make a judgment about the value of this option. Once more we find that Nature's tree of Figure 1.6 supplies the probabilistic information we require. The probabilities of the branches D_1 and D_1' that leave node T_3 have already been computed in the tree for test plan T_1; they are 0.2 and 0.8. The only remaining probabilities are $Pr(D_2|D_1)$ and $Pr(D_2'|D_1)$ to go to the right of node T_3D_1 CONTINUE and the probabilities $Pr(D_2|D_1')$ and $Pr(D_2'|D_1')$ to go in the analogous place on the D_1' fork. Our task is again simplified by the fact that the sum of all probabilities emerging from a chance node must be 1. By rearrangement of the Product Rule we can write:

$$Pr(D_2|D_1) = Pr(D_1D_2)Pr(D_1)$$

and

$$Pr(D_2|D_1') = Pr(D_2D_1') = Pr(D_2'D_2)/Pr(D_1')$$

From Figure 1.6 we find

$$Pr(D_2|D_1) = \frac{Pr(D_1D_2)}{Pr(D_1)} = \frac{Pr(PD_1D_2) + Pr(LD_1D_2}{Pr(PD_1D_2) + Pr(LD_1D_2) + Pr(LD_1D_2) + Pr(PD_1D_2) + Pr(LD_1D_2)}$$

$$= \frac{.067}{12} = .33$$

and

$$Pr(D_2|D_1') = \frac{Pr(D_1'D_2)}{Pr(D_1)} = \frac{Pr(PD_1'D_2) + Pr(LD_1'D_2)}{Pr(PD_1'D_2) + Pr(LD_1'D_2) + Pr(PD_1'D_2' + Pr(D_1'D_2')}$$

$$= .134/.8 = .166$$

Of course, most of the probabilities in this calculation were computed earlier in the evaluation of test options T_1 and T_2. However, their repetition at this time serves to emphasize the basic role of Nature's tree. Finally, we have

$$Pr(D_2'|D_1) = 1 - Pr(D_2|D_1) = .667$$

38

and

$$Pr(D_2' \mid D_1') = 1 - Pr(D_2 \mid D_1') = .833$$

When the four conditional probabilities we have just found are entered in their appropriate places in the tree for test option T_3, we are ready to proceed with the expected value computation.

At node $T_3 D_1'$ CONTINUE there is a 1/3 probability of the value 40K and a 2/3 probability of the value 28K. The expected value of this node is thus $1/3(40)+2/3(28)=\$32K$, as indicated in the square box. The node $T_3 D_1$ STOP also has a value of $32K$, however, in order to reach node $T_3 D_1$ CONTINUE $4K must be paid and so, when viewed from the left end of the $T_3 D_1$ CONTINUE branch, this action is worth only $28K. Consequently, Joe is best advised to take the STOP branch at this juncture and thereby make the value of decision node $T_3 D_1$ equal to $32K. Such a decision has been indicated on the tree.

At node $T_3 D_1'$ CONTINUE we see a 1/6 probability of the value $28K and a 5/6 probability of the value $53,600. The expected value of node $T_3 D_1'$ CONTINUE is $1/6(28,000)+5/6(53,600)=\$49,330$. Even after the $4,000 expense for continuing the test has been included, this act still has an expected value of $45,330, an amount slightly in excess of the $44K value to be expected if branch $T_3 D_1$ STOP is followed. The solid arrowhead and the number at node $T_3 D_1'$ correspond to this decision.

At chance node T_3 there is an 0.2 probability of the yard's reporting that it found a defect on the test, resulting in an EMV of $32K. On the other hand, with probability 0.8 Joe will have an EMV of $45,330 because it has reported no defect. Therefore, the expected value of being at decision node T_3 is $0.2(32,000)+0.8(45,330)=\$43,660$. Since it is necessary to pay $10K for the first test, the expected value of test plan T_3 is $32,660.

We have now evaluated all four test plans. From Figure 1.4 we can see that the EMV's associated with the options $T_0, T_1,$

T_2 and T_3 are, respectively, $28,000, $32,600, $32,870, and $32,660. Since plan T_2--that of testing two systems--has the highest EMV, it is the one indicated by a solid arrowhead after the initial decision node. However, the evidence of the tree should be interpreted not to mean that T_2 is the best test plan, but rather that any of the plans T_1, T_2, T_3 will be slightly less than $5K better than the option of no testing on the average. The big payoff is not in the selection of a particular test plan, but rather in the decision to do some testing.

Let us review these test plans to show their operational character. If Joe does no testing, he will buy the ship without a guarantee. If he follows plan T_1, he will buy the ship with the guarantee if a defect is found in the system tested, and he will buy it without the guarantee if no defect is discovered. Our evaluation of plan T_2 shows that Joe should buy the ship without a guarantee only if no defects are found in the two systems tested, and buy it with the guarantee otherwise. Finally, if T_3 is chosen, Joe should stop further testing if a defect is discovered on the first test and continue testing otherwise. If a defect is found in the first test on the turbine, then Joe should buy the ship with a guarantee, as we see from the decision at node T_2D_1. However, if the turbine is not defective, then, depending on whether the further test of the gear does or does not reveal a defect, Joe will either buy the ship with or without a guarantee, respectively. This is determined by locating the ultimate outcomes of the T_3D_1' CONTINUE D_2 and T_3D_1' CONTINUE D_2' branches in the T_2 tree. It is interesting to note that the reason the nodes T_3D_1 CONTINUE and T_3D_1 STOP have the same value is that, even if the tests were continued at this point, Joe's decision would be to buy the ship with a guarantee regardless of how the second test came out. Since the test cannot affect the decision, it is not worthwhile to pay anything for the privilege of making it. The tree implies just this result.

We have now seen that after all the calculations have been

performed the final decision offers no real problem. Since test plan T_2 is most favorable by a small amount, Joe will probably decide to follow it. The expected value of perfect information is $23,130 when plan T_2 is used; therefore, the stranger's $25,000 price for this information once more looks too high. Unless the price is lowered below $23,130, Joe should proceed with having the fuel and electrical systems tested at a cost of $13K. He will buy the ship without the guarantee only if no defects are found, and with it otherwise. Joe's expected gain from this plan of action is $32,870, an increase of $4,870 over what he expected to make without considering testing.

The stranger with the perfect information has witnessed a good deal of vacillation in what Joe is willing to pay him. The EVPI was $20K initially, $28K after the guarantee was introduced, and $23,130 under test plan T_2. From the stranger's point of view, the guarantee was good news, but the test options were bad news.

Well, at last Joe is putting out to sea in his newly-acquired C4, having used test plan T_2 and abided by the results. A most human question is: did he make a good decision or didn't he? The answer to this question does not depend at all on whether his ship is actually a peach or a lemon. We must make a distinction between a good decision and a good outcome. Joe made a good decision because he based it on logic and his available knowledge. Whether or not the outcome is good depends on the vagaries of chance. Psychologically, perhaps the most basic difference between decision-making under certainty and decision-making under uncertainty is that in decision-making under uncertainty you cannot judge a decision by its outcome. Chapter 2 will attempt to place this contention on a solid foundation.

CHAPTER 2

BAYESIAN DECISION THEORY

Chapter 2 is divided into two parts. The first part attempts to give a persuasive, non-formal presentation of the Bayesian approach to decisions under uncertainty. The second part is a reasonably complete statement of the axioms of decision theory and a proof that, if the DM accepts these axioms, he can and indeed logically must analyze decisions under uncertainty in the manner outlined in Part I if he is to be consistent with these axioms. While Part II is hardly fun reading, it is not difficult and we urge all readers, including those unused to axiomatic reasoning, to wade through it, for it forms the logical basis for all the hopefully more interesting marine applications that follow.

PART I.   A NON-FORMAL PRESENTATION OF DECISION THEORY

INTRODUCTION

Our study of Joe's dilemma begged two extremely important questions which lie at the core of decision-making under uncertainty.

1.   In the real world, the likelihoods of future events are not generally immediately available even if one eavesdrops on one's broker. Question: how does one come up with the needed probabilities when they are not handed to you?

2.   In the real world, most people are not EMV'ers. If all DM's were expected value decision-makers, we would have no insurance companies. There would be little need for risk-sharing institutions such as venture capital corporations or offshore exploration syndicates. If oil companies or, for that matter, any large shippers were expected value decision-makers, there would be no point in obtaining their transportation requirements from a mix of own ships, term charters and voyage charters. People in general and marine investors and operators

in particular are rarely EMV'ers, and with good reason.* Our
job is to develop a methodology for obtaining decisions which
are consistent with the DM's values, not to tell him what these
values should be. Hence, there is no getting around the question: what should one do if one is not an EMV'er?

---

*Expected value decision-making can lead to some rather strange
choices in many situations. Consider the case of the horse-
race fixer. Suppose there are N horses in a race and, due to
certain medical ministrations which you have accomplished, you
believe the probability of the nth horse's winning is p_n. The
betting public is not aware of your thoughtful care for the
equines and bets the horses in such a way that the parimutual
odds (return for dollar invested in nth horse if it wins) is r_n.
Suppose you are an EMV'er with total capital of C dollars. Let
$x_n \geq 0$ be the amount bet on the nth horse. Then your problem is
to distribute all or a portion of your capital over the N horses
in such a way as to:

$$\max_{\{x_n\}} \sum_{n=1}^{N} p_n r_n x_n$$

subject to

$$\sum_{n=1}^{N} x_n \leq C$$

This simple constrained optimization problem belongs to a class
of problems known as linear programs. From basic linear programming theory, one can easily show that the solution of this
problem is to bet all your capital on the horse with the highest
$p_n r_n$. This solution will maximize your expected winnings. It
also has a very high probability of ruin. In fact, if one follows this strategy over a large number of races, your expected
value goes to infinity while the probability of ruin goes to 1.
Not many people would want to follow such a strategy, especially when it can be shown that there exist other strategies
for distribution of your bets among the horses which will effect a positive expected rate of growth of your capital while
guaranteeing that you will never go broke. See reference 7.
Another historically famous situation in which EMVing leads to
rather strange results is the so-called St. Petersburg Paradox.
See reference 16.

43

Putting aside for the moment our nagging worries about where do you get the probabilities, we will take the second question first. Suppose now that our friend Joe falls into that large class of people, the non-EMV'ers, people who would be delighted, for example, to accept $48,000 in exchange for a 50-50 chance at $0 or $100,000. What can Joe salvage from his earlier analysis? Well, he can still draw the decision tree, put the monetary payoffs at the terminal nodes and, since we are accepting for the moment his probabilities, he can still assign the same probabilities on the branches coming out of the chance nodes. The trouble is that, if Joe is a non-EMV'er, he can no longer fold the tree back taking expectations of the monetary results at chance nodes and maximizing EMV's at decision nodes.

At this point, our brilliant friend Joe has another of his brainstorms. He says to himself, "The trouble is that the reason why I am not indifferent between, say, 50,000 for sure and a 50-50 chance at 0 or 100,000 dollars is that in some sense obtaining 0 dollars is a lot worse relative to 50,000 than getting 100,000 dollars is good. What I need is a way of calibrating my differential feelings toward the different monetary outcomes."

Now there are any number of ways Joe might calibrate his feelings about the monetary outcomes open to him. The way that we are about to suggest will seem at first strange, but later we will see it has a very surprising and important property.

Joe says to himself, "What I have got to do is ask myself a set of questions about how I feel about the various monetary outcomes which *a priori* might result from the courses of action open to me." Reviewing these outcomes, he notes that they range from a high +$60,000 (no test, buy without guarantee and ship is peach) to a low of -$114,000 (use both tests of T_3, buy without guarantee, and ship is lemon). Joe continues, "Suppose I construct a set of gambles or lotteries which have only two possible outcomes. One outcome which I'll call W (for win) is

44

a prize of $60,000; the other outcome L (for lose) is the loss
of $114,000. Now, for any monetary outcome between $60K and
-$114,000, say, x dollars I could ask myself the following
question: For what chance π between 0 and 1 would I be indifferent between x dollars for sure and the gamble which gives
me a π chance at W(60K) and a 1-π chance at L(-$114K)?" That
is, Joe constructs the following little decision tree:

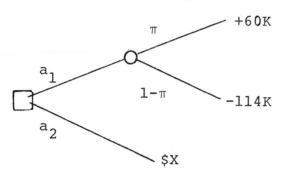

One may regard the upper left-hand branch in this tree, a_1,
which, if taken, yields as a prize the nontransferable rights
to participate in a game of chance in which the outcome is
either W(60K) or L(-$114K). These rights might take the form
of a lottery ticket. The ticket might be a little card on which
would be inscribed "This card entitles the bearer to a lottery
which yields a π chance at W and a 1-π chance at L." On the
actual card, π would be a number between 0 and 1.* We shall
call such a prize a basic reference lottery ticket or, for short,
a BRLT; read "brilt" and not "b,r,l,t." Using this definition,
alternative a_2 of our little tree yields a π-BRLT and a shorthand way of drawing this tree is:

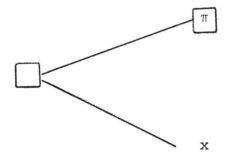

---

*In Joe's case W is the gain of $60,000 and L is the loss of
$114,000. But all you really have to keep in mind about W
and L is that they are precisely defined consequences such
that W is clearly preferred to L.

where the boxed π indicates that the consequence of the upper branch is π-BRLT.

Clearly, a 1.0-BRLT is identical to W and 0.0-BRLT is the same as L. Also, clearly, as long as consequence W is preferred to consequence L, it would be reasonable to assume that any DM given a choice between two different BRLT's would always prefer the one with the higher chance at the preferred price, the one with the higher π value.

This last sentence would seem to be an innocent enough statement, but it has a very important and subtle implication. Suppose a DM subscribing to this statement, say yourself, were faced with the following choice:

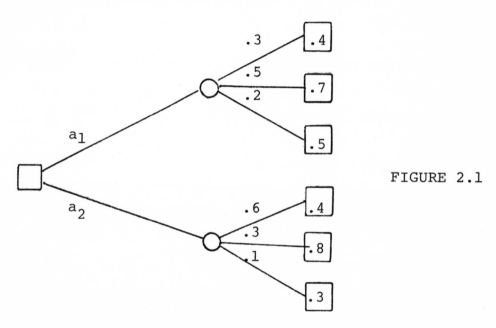

FIGURE 2.1

If you choose either alternative a_1 or alternative a_2, you will be confronted with a lottery whose prizes are basic reference lottery tickets.* Consider the gamble associated with a_1. We can make the nature of this chance node clear if we proceed as follows. Imagine an urn containing 30 green balls, 50 yellow balls and 20 orange balls. If we decide on alternative a_1, our old friend Nature will pick a ball from this urn. If it

---

*The following argument is based closely upon reference 17, Chapter 4.

46

is green, we proceed to a .4-BRLT, if yellow, to a .7-BRLT, and if orange, to a .5-BRLT. That is, a green ball means that Nature will move to another urn which contains 40 balls marked W and 60 balls marked L from which she will draw a second ball which determines whether you end up with a W or with an L. Similarly, a yellow ball on the first drawing means she goes to an urn in which .7 of the balls are marked W; an orange ball means she goes to an urn in which half the balls are marked W.

Nature could proceed in another fashion which, for all practical purposes, is equivalent to the above process. Suppose she places a total of 100 balls in a single urn, the composition being 30 green, 50 yellow and 20 orange as before. This time, however, she labels 12 of the green balls with a W and the other 18 with an L. That is, .4 of the green balls are labeled W. Similarly, she labels .7 of the yellow balls (35 of them) with a W and the rest with an L. Finally, she marks half of the orange balls with a W and the other 10 with an L. She now draws a single ball at random from the urn, observes the color, and states immediately whether it is a W or an L and gives you the corresponding consequence. Of course, the color is irrelevant. The important fact is the number of W 's in this urn. Since there are 12 + 35 + 10 = 57 W's and 43 L's, drawing from this urn is exactly equivalent to a .57-BRLT. We conclude, therefore, that the gamble associated with a_1 is equivalent to (or reducible to) a .57-BRLT. Observe that .3 × .4 + .5 × .7 + .2 × .5 = .57. That is, .57 is the weighted average of the ticket numbers .4, .7, and .5 where the weights are the probabilities on the respective branches. Or, using our definition of expected value, .57 is the expectation of the BRLT values or the expected BRLT value. In a similar fashion, you can verify that the chance node associated with alternative a_2 is reducible to a .51-BRLT. So

47

your choice boils down to either a .57-BRLT or a .51-BRLT. Clearly, your choice should be a_1 and the whole venture is now worth a .57-BRLT.

It is extremely important that you realize what we have just demonstrated. At first blush, one might have felt that it is no more appropriate for non-EMV'ers to use the expected value of the BRLT numbers than it was appropriate for them to use expected monetary values that, for example, some allowance must be made for how widely the BRLT values are spread in a_1 versus a_2. This is not so. Review once again the argument of the last two pages. It says that it is appropriate to use the expected value of the BRLT numbers without any allowance for the spread of these numbers. Further, this is true even though it's understood that this lottery will be conducted just once and not repeated. Finally and most importantly, it is true no matter whether you are an EMV'er or a non-EMV'er, whether you like risk or are risk-adverse. Regardless of what monetary equivalent you associate with the basic reference prizes, once you are faced with a decision in which all the results are reference lotteries, it is appropriate to base your decisions on the average value of the BRLT's. This would not be true if the prizes were monetary values.

Well, I hope you can now see the way we are pushing our poor friend Joe. For if for each of the possible monetary outcomes x which might occur in his problem he can find a BRLT value $\pi(x)$ such that he is indifferent between x dollars for sure and the basic reference lottery in which outcome W has a chance of $\pi(x)$, then we could replace each monetary outcome with the equivalent basic reference lottery ticket. After we have replaced the monetary outcomes with their BRLT values Joe will face choices of the same type as those shown in Figure 2-1 in which all the paths lead eventually to a BRLT. Hence, we can fold this tree back using expectation on the BRLT values in exactly the same manner as he used expectation on the monetary outcomes when he was an EMV'er.

48

2.2 JOE'S PREFERENCE FUNCTION

Let us see how Joe might go about assigning π-values to the various monetary outcomes which can result from his choices. The first thing Joe has to do is decide on a W and an L, on two monetary values that are sufficiently far apart that they encompass all the possible outcomes in his problem. As indicated earlier he could pick W='gain of 60K' and L='loss of 114K', or he could pick any W higher than +60K and any L lower than -114K. We shall see that it doesn't matter as long as he sticks with the same W and the same L throughout his analysis of the problem. Let us say he goes with a W of +100K and L of -150K just so he can deal with even numbers. In short, for Joe we introduce the set of basic reference lotteries in which the more preferred consequence is a gain of $100K and the less preferred consequence is a loss of $150K. In other words, a π-BRLT gives Joe a π chance at +100K and 1-π chance at -150K.

Next we ask Joe what amount x he would want for certain in lieu of a π-BRLT for all possible π's. His answers set up a correspondence between x and π. We can graph this correspondence in the form of a curve where for each x on the abscissa there is a corresponding π(x) on the ordinate. Figure 2-2 is such a graph. This curve is called a preference curve for money and completely characterizes Joe's evaluation of the possible consequences which could befall him. Thus, for example, on the graph shown the point (-60,.67) lies on the curve which means that Joe is indifferent between losing 60K for sure and a .67 chance at +100K and a complementary chance at -$150. Clearly, Joe is now very risk-adverse.

Even before we ask Joe any questions, we know two points on this curve since, by definition, a 1.0-BRLT is the same as +$100K for sure and 0.0-BRLT is the same as a loss of $150K for sure, the curve must go through the points (100K,1.0) and (-150K,0.0). In fact, the preference curve for an EMV'er is simply a straight line between these two points. We can verify this by going back to our little tree on page 45 and observing that for an EMV'er

$$x = \pi(x)(100K) + (1-\pi(x))(-150K)$$

$$\pi(x) = (x+150K)/250K$$

which is just the equation of a straight line between the two end points. However, Joe is no longer an EMV'er and, therefore, we will have to get him to reveal his preference function by asking him a set of appropriate questions. For example, we might ask him at what π he would be indifferent between $0 for sure (the status quo) and a π-chance at the reference prizes. Suppose, after considerable soul-searching, he answers he would not be willing to give up the status quo unless he obtained a .9 chance at the gain of $100K. If this is the case, the point (0K,.9) is on Joe's curve. (This is point #1 in the graph.) We might then ask Joe at what x he would be indifferent between the alternatives a_1 and a_2 in the following tree.

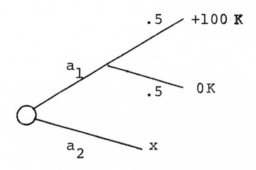

Suppose he said $40K. Well, the upper branch is reducible to a .95-BRLT. Hence, .95 must be the BRLT value associated with +40K. This is point #2 in the Figure 2.2. Continuing in like manner, we might ask Joe for the amount of x for which he would be indifferent between the following two alternatives.

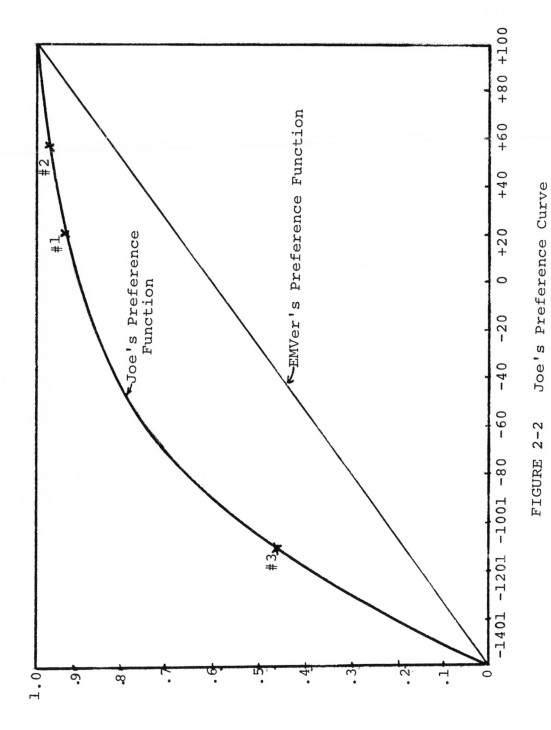

FIGURE 2-2   Joe's Preference Curve

51

Suppose he answers that he would pay 110,000 dollars to avoid this unfavorable gamble. Then (-110K,.45) is on Joe's curve since the top half of this tree reduces to a .45-BRLT. We now have five points on Joe's preference function.

In serious business matters, many individuals are risk-adverse in the sense that for any lottery of the form

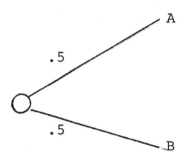

where y and z are specific monetary amounts, the amount x for which they would be indifferent between this lottery and x for sure is less than the EMV of the lottery or

$$x < .5y + .5z$$

It is an easy matter to show that if an individual is risk-adverse in this sense, his preference function must be concave, i.e., shaped like this ⌒ and not like ⌣ . Thus, if Joe regards himself as risk-adverse, he will want to fit a curve through the points we have obtained for him which is always curving to the right as we proceed northeastward along it. We have fitted such a curve through the points we have obtained in Figure 2-2. Joe should now test this curve by looking at different lotteries of the form

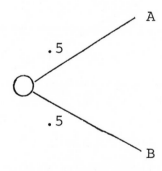

for a variety of values of y and z

and determining the amount x for which he would be indifferent
between x for sure and the lottery and then seeing if the point
(x,.5y+.5z) is on the curve. Occasionally, the results will
not jibe and Joe will have to bend or straighten out the curve.
Let us assume that, after such jockeying, he ends up with the
curve as it is drawn in Figure 2.2.

At this point, Joe can turn the analysis of his problem
back to us, saying, "I don't know what my best strategy is, but
I want it to be consistent with this preference function."
If that is the case, we can proceed as follows.

First, we replace all the monetary values associated with
traversing any path in the tree by their corresponding indifference values. This has been done in Figure 2.3. Notice
we must perform this substitution with the final outcome including any payments for testing or guarantees made before the
final branching points in the tree. In folding the tree back,
we no longer have the freedom of not counting a payment until
we reach the point on the tree where the payment is actually
made. The only reason we got away with this before is that the
EMV of the sum of two monetary payments (rewards) is equal to
the sum of the EMV of each individual gain (loss). This is not
true for BRLT values. A payment, say for a guarantee, changes
your asset position which in general changes your whole outlook
on the risks you are willing to take. We must throw all payments and gains to their rightmost nodes, and only then apply
the BRLT values and begin folding back.

Let us actually do just one of the possible test plans,
say T_3. In order to do so, we will assume that Joe's preference function is given by the graph in Figure 2.2, which is
closely approximated by

$$\pi(x)=.13(1-.5^{.02x})+.90$$

where x is the monetary outcome in thousands of dollars. Using
this approximation the π-values associated with each of the

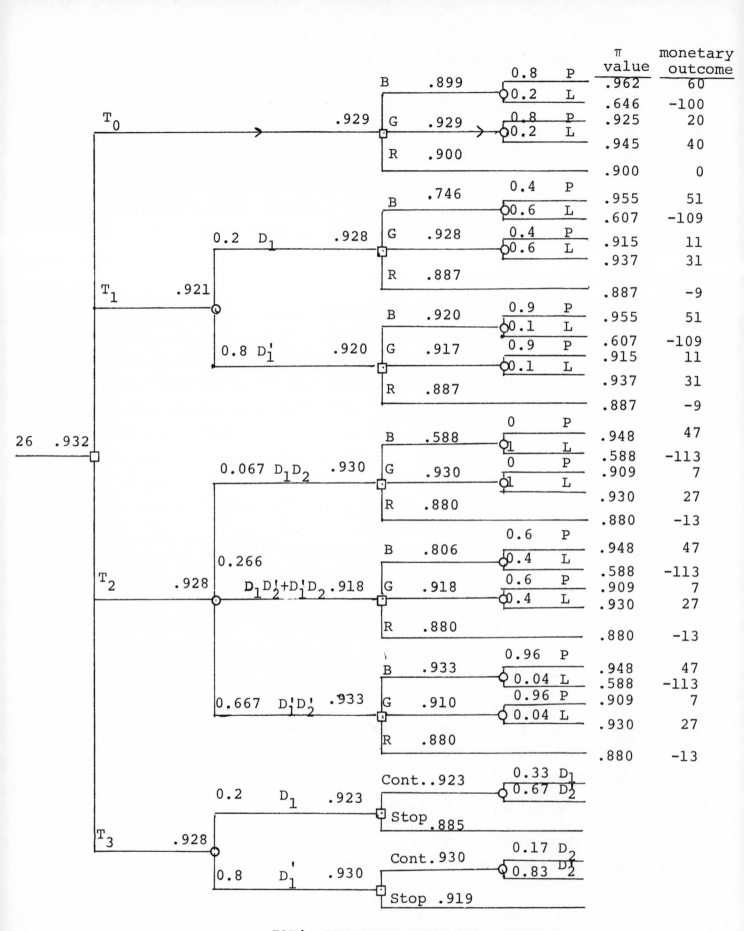

JOE's DECISION TREE WITH UTILITY
FIGURE 2-3

54

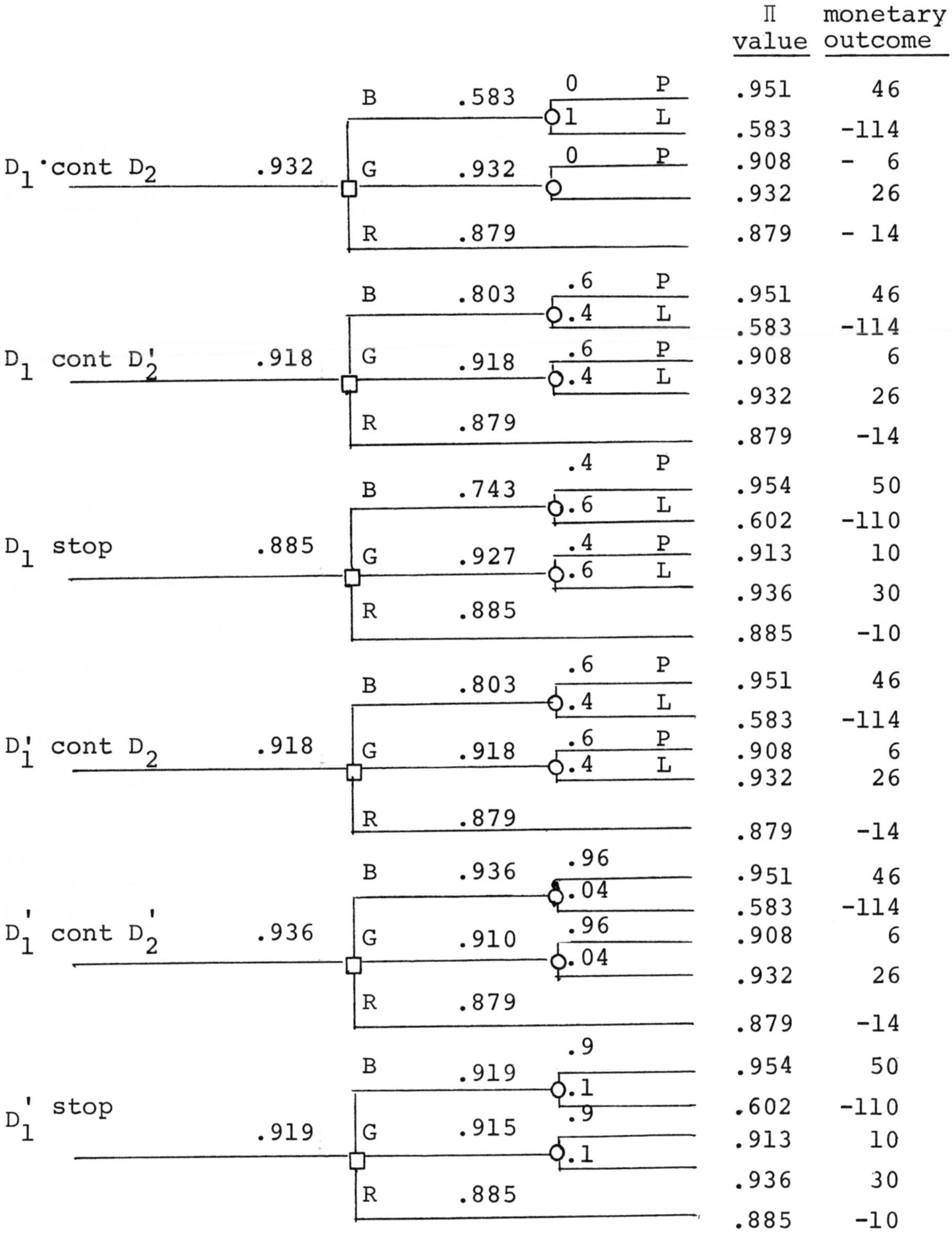

					Π value	monetary outcome

$D_1 \cdot$ cont D_2 .932

B .583 — 0 — P → .951 — 46
1 — L → .583 — −114
G .932 — 0 — P → .908 — − 6
.932 — 26
R .879 → .879 — − 14

D_1 cont D_2' .918

B .803 — .6 — P → .951 — 46
.4 — L → .583 — −114
G .918 — .6 — P → .908 — 6
.4 — L → .932 — 26
R .879 → .879 — −14

D_1 stop .885

B .743 — .4 — P → .954 — 50
.6 — L → .602 — −110
G .927 — .4 — P → .913 — 10
.6 — L → .936 — 30
R .885 → .885 — −10

D_1' cont D_2 .918

B .803 — .6 — P → .951 — 46
.4 — L → .583 — −114
G .918 — .6 — P → .908 — 6
.4 — L → .932 — 26
R .879 → .879 — −14

D_1' cont D_2' .936

B .936 — .96 → .951 — 46
.04 → .583 — −114
G .910 — .96 → .908 — 6
.04 → .932 — 26
R .879 → .879 — −14

D_1' stop .919

B .919 — .9 → .954 — 50
.1 → .602 — −110
G .915 — .9 → .913 — 10
.1 → .936 — 30
R .885 → .885 — −10

CONTINUATION OF JOE'S TREE FOR TEST PLAN T_3

FIGURE 2-3a

possible outcomes of test plan T_3 are shown if Figure 2.3.*
Notice that the monetary outcomes include *all* the rewards and
penalties associated with moving along the path leading to each
node. Folding the preference function back leads to the node
values shown at the left-hand side of Figure 2.3a. At any
point in the tree we can obtain the monetary amount for which
the DM would be willing to sell the rights he has at that node,
i.e., the amount x for which he is indifferent between x dollars for sure and the lottery which he faces at the particular
node. This quantity is called the *certainty monetary equivalent* (CME) of the node and the CME for the leftmost nodes in
this subtree has been placed under the corresponding node.

The remainder of the folding-back process has been carried
through completely in Figure 2.3. Notice that the new optimal
strategy is not to test at all but to buy the ship immediately
with the guarantee. The reason for this is that our friend Joe
is so risk-adverse that he ends up buying with the guarantee
almost no matter what happens in any test plan. If you almost
always are going to end up buying with the guarantee no matter
what the outcome of the test, there is little point in paying
for a test.

Joe can still figure out how much he should be willing to
pay the stranger for his information at any node, N, by solving
the following expression for y.

---

*Actually, since we are going to take expected values of the
preference function and expectation is a linear operation,
one could use any positive linear transformation of the preference function and obtain the same strategy. For example,
it would be a little simpler in Joe's case if we worked with
the function $1-.5^{.02x}$. A function which is a positive linear
transformation of a preference function is known as a Von Neumann-
Morgenstern utility. See reference 20.

Pr(Stranger says Peach|Information available at node N)

π(Monetary amount he can make if ship is a peach
given his present position -y

+Pr(Stranger says Lemon|Information at node N)

π(Monetary amount he can make if ship is a lemon
given his present position -y)

=π(Node N)

The left-hand side of this expression is the expected value of his preference function given that he pays the stranger amount y. The right-hand side is the expected value of the preference function given that he does the best he can without the stranger's information. The maximum amount, y, he should pay the stranger is the amount which leaves him indifferent between having the information and not having it. Notice in general there is no direct relationship between the CME of a node and the value of perfect information as there was for the EMV'er.

2.3   WHERE DO WE GET THE PROBABILITIES?

We are now ready to turn to the problem of where do we get the probabilities we need in order to fold the decision tree back in that very large set of real-life cases where there is no "firm" data upon which to base probabilities. Consider, for example, an offshore wildcatter who is thinking about an expensive seismic survey in a previously-unexplored area. No data on the area exists and all his geologist will say is, "Geologically, the region has some resemblance to the Black Sea and there have been some finds there, but it also resembles the Bay of Bengal and nobody has found any oil there." What does this man use for the probabilities of the possible outcomes of his tests? Or consider a shipowner wondering whether or not he should introduce a new technology, say a new power plant, aboard his ships. If the plant is as good as the manufacturer's claim, he will have a definite competitive advantage over his colleagues, but the owner knows that new plants are rarely as good as the manufacturer's claim, at least not at first. No real operational data exists on the plant. How can this man

57

obtain the probabilities he needs to analyze his decision tree? Other examples: the probability that the Suez Canal will reopen in 1972, the probability that the North Sea will be producing x billion barrels of oil in 1974 for a range of x.

In order to indicate how a DM might approach this difficult set of problems, let us return once again to Joe's problem with the following variation.

> A shipowner named Joe of our acquaintance is in the market for a used C-4. After surveying a number of brokers, he has found one such ship for one million dollars. The best deal he can get elsewhere is $1.1 million for a fully found ship. Joe likes the looks of this ship and figures he will save $100,000 by buying it. Unfortunately, just as Joe is about to close the deal, he overhears the broker who has been serving him talking with another broker. His broker says, "This business is a tough racket. I have a buyer for that old C-4, but the practices of our business prevent me from warning him that he may get stuck if he buys it." The other broker asks, "What do you mean?" Joe's broker replies, "I used to work for the company that built that ship. Some, I don't know how many, of this class were built in a new yard where they were still having production problems, those ships were lemons. The rest were pretty good ships; peaches, we used to call them...

Joe's problem now is that, while he realizes that the probability of his ship's being a peach is crucial to his analysis, he has no firm data, such as the ratio of peaches to lemons, upon which to base this probability. Joe knows that the shipbuilder is unlikely to tell him how many lemons it made and that the broker is sure to claim that it is a peach, if asked. In fact, in the time available Joe doesn't have anything to go on other than his general impressions about how this class has performed in the past. Of course, these impressions are based on long experience in the business, years of using his judgment to sift and combine rumor, hearsay, and hard facts relating to these ships. Joe certainly doesn't want to throw this hard-won experience out the window. In fact, he regards his intuitive knowledge of ships and shipping as his most valuable asset. The problem, rather, is to incorporate this set of experiences into the analysis.

In order to do so, he will have to calibrate his vague feelings about the likelihood that his ship is a peach. How can he perform this calibration? Well, after his earlier luck with BRLT's Joe decides that maybe by asking himself the right set of questions concerning basic reference lotteries, he can measure his judgments concerning the likelihood that the ship is a peach. Joe sets up the following tree.

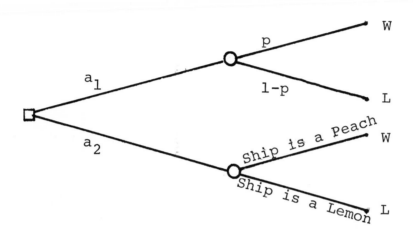

The upper branch resulting from taking alternative a_1 leads to a p-BRLT. That is, a lottery which has p chance of consequence W and 1-p chance of consequence L. (We can use any W and L we like as long as W is preferred to L.) Alternative a_2, on the other hand, leads to a lottery which awards consequence W if the ship is in fact a peach and consequence L if the ship is a lemon. Now Joe asks himself which of the alternatives he prefers, which of these lotteries he would rather have. Clearly, if p is very close to 1.0, he will prefer a_1 if he has any substantial doubts at all about the ship's true character. By the same token, if p is very close to 0, he will prefer a_2, the alternative leading to the lottery based on the real-world event. At some intermediate value of p, Joe will have a very difficult time deciding between the two options. After a great deal of soul-searching based on his long experience with these ships, Joe might conclude that anywhere between p=.75 and p=.85 he is substantially indifferent between a_1 and a_2. p=.8 is a central value in the range of Joe's indecision, so let us assume Joe agrees that he is indifferent between a_2 and a .8-BRLT.

The question then is to what extent we can regard .8 as Joe's probability that the ship is a peach. Should Joe, given the above indifference, analyze his problem just as if he knew that the proportion of peaches was 80%? Should he update this calibrated judgment via Bayes rule as he did before, given the results of his test plans? Should he act in all ways just as if this .8 was just as good a probability as the earlier .8 based on knowing the proportions? The answer is yes, provided:

a) Joe wants his decisions to be consistent with a set of postulates which we are about to present.

b) Joe has no other means than the ones already postulated for obtaining information on the ship's true status.*

However, in order to present this argument we are going to have to go back to the beginning and carefully lay out just what postulates concerning decision-making under uncertainty Joe will have to accept in order to make this statement true. We will call these postulates axioms and each DM will have to decide for himself whether or not he wants his choices to obey these axioms. If the answer is yes, we will be able to prove not only that the DM can determine *his* probabilities in the manner outlined above, but also that if he does so and if he determines his preference function as indicated earlier, then logically he must fold back any decision tree he faces in the manner we have suggested and follow the indicated strategy.

---

*If there were a means other than those displayed in the decision tree of Figure 2.3 by which Joe could obtain more information about the likelihood of a peach, then the problem becomes strategically different from the Chapter I problem with a different tree. For example, if Joe knew that the broker knew what the proportion of peaches was, Joe can now reasonably consider such strategies as offering the broker a bribe for the information and develop the decision tree relevant to determining how large a bribe he could advantageously offer. In the original problem, since Joe already was certain of this proportion, it made no sense to consider paying for this information.

PART II. THE FOUNDATIONS OF DECISION THEORY

2.4 THE BASIC PROBLEM

Any decision under uncertainty, however complex, can be boiled down to the following core problem: A DM is faced with a choice between two risky alternatives or lotteries, ℓ and ℓ'. ℓ will award the DM consequence c_i if event E_i occurs and ℓ' will award the DM c_i' if E_i' occurs. These alternatives are sketched below. The sets $\{E_i\}$ and $\{E_i'\}$ must each be mutually exclusive and collectively exhaustive. Any decision under uncertainty can be reduced to this problem in the sense that, if we can handle this choice, we can solve any more complex problem.

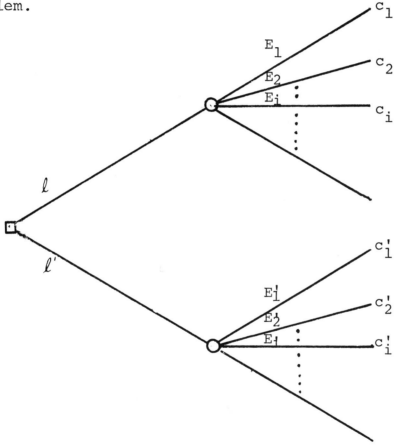

Decision theory is that branch of systems analysis which has developed to handle precisely this problem. Decision theory is based on the *fact* that if the DM is willing to scale his

61

preferences for the possible consequences of his actions and his judgments concerning the uncertain events which will affect the outcome of his actions and is willing to accept two principles of consistent behavior, then he can by straightforward calculation determine which of several risky alternatives he should adopt if he is to be consistent with his own preferences and judgments.

2.5 CANONICAL CHANCE

In order to give the DM a basis upon which to quantify his preferences and judgments, we must introduce the concept of a canonical lottery. A canonical lottery is a lottery in which, *as far as the DM is concerned*, all the possible outcomes are equally likely. Consider an experiment with N possible outcomes and consider two lotteries $\ell*$ and $\ell**$. $\ell*$ awards a valuable consequence c if the result of the experiment is any of $n*$ of the possible outcomes of the experiment, and $\ell**$ awards the same consequence if any of $n**$ of the possible outcomes occur.
If DM prefers $\ell*$ to $\ell**$, if and only if $n*>n**$, then we say the experiment is *canonical*. If DM is indifferent to the exact designation of the outcomes in this manner, we say that the outcomes are *equally likely*. A *canonical lottery* is any lottery in which the consequence will be determined by a canonical experiment. Finally, we call the ratio of the number of outcomes leading to consequence $\gamma, n(\gamma)$; in a canonical lottery to the total number of possible outcomes the *canonical chance* of γ.

> Very roughly, a canonical experiment is an experiment
> in which all the possible outcomes are equally likely.
> Notice that our definition of equally likely depends
> on the DM and his indifferences. Thus, what may be
> a canonical experiment to one DM will not be a canoni-
> cal experiment to another DM. There is no vague appeal
> to symmetry in this definition of equally likely.

Theorem: Canonical chance as defined above is a probability measure on the sample space of the outcomes of the canonical experiment.

At this point, we must indicate just what we mean by a probability measure. That is, we must tighten up our somewhat loose use of the word "probability." To a mathematician probabilities are numbers assigned to events which obey the following three simple rules:

1) For any event A, $Pr(A) \geq 0$

2) $Pr(A+A') = 1.00$

3) If A and B are mutually exclusive, then
   $Pr(A+B) = Pr(A) + Pr(B)$

Surprisingly, all of probability theory including the Sum Rule, the Product Rule and Bayes Rule can be derived from these rules.

Thus, in order to prove that canonical chance as defined above is a probability, it is only necessary to show that $n(\gamma)/N$ obey these three rules. But that is almost obvious.

1) The ratio of a non-negative number, $n(\gamma)$ and another non-negative number, N, is non-negative.

2) The consequence $\gamma + \gamma'$ is the consequence of all the possible outcomes. By the above description, the canonical chance of any of the possible outcomes is $N/N = 1$.

3) Let γ_1 and γ_2 be two possible sets of outcomes such that γ_1 and γ_2 cannot occur simultaneously, then the number of outcomes favorable to the consequence $(\gamma_1 + \gamma_2)$ is equal to $n(\gamma_1) + n(\gamma_2)$. Hence, the canonical chance of $\gamma_1 + \gamma_2$ equals the canonical chance of γ_1 plus the canonical chance of γ_2.

In short, canonical chances are probabilities which means, among other things, we can combine them according to the Sum Rule.

We are now ready to state Axiom I. In order to obtain a meaningful basis for quantification of preferences and judgments, we must assume that, for any pair of real-world consequences, the DM can imagine a canonical experiment whose outcome will determine which of these consequences he will receive. Further, given two such canonical lotteries, he will prefer the one which gives him the higher canonical chance at the more preferred consequence. More precisely:

Axiom I. Let c' and c" by any real-world consequences such that c'≻c".* For any positive integer N, the decision-maker can postulate an experiment with N possible outcomes such that, if one lottery entitles him to c' on the occurrence of one of n' possible outcomes and c" otherwise, while another lottery entitles him to c" on the occurrence of one of n" possible outcomes, then DM will prefer the former lottery to the latter if and only if n'>n'.

> The reader should observe that Axiom I implies that the outcomes of this experiment are equally likely in the sense defined above and, thus, the experiment so postulated is canonical. Axiom I implies not only the existence of a canonical lottery, but also that canonical lotteries with the same pair of prizes can be ranked according to the canonical chance that they yield of obtaining the more preferred consequence. As we shall see, Axiom I gives us a fully defined reference scale for measuring our subjective preferences and judgments.

Axiom II postulates the decision-maker's ability to rank his preferences for the set of possible consequences in terms of canonical lotteries.

Axiom II. Given any set on consequences, $\{c_i\}$, the DM can select a consequence c* which he finds at least as attractive, and another consequence, c_*, which he finds at least as unattractive as any other of the consequences. Further, he can quantify his preference for each of the possible consequences c_i by specifying a number $\pi(c_i)$ between 0 and 1 such that he would be indifferent between c for certain and a lottery yielding a canonical chance $\pi(c_i)$ at c* and a complementary chance at c_*.

> Thus we ask the DM to display his preferences for the possible consequences by considering the set of alternatives sketched below

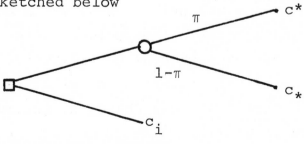

*The symbol "≻" is shorthand for "is preferred to." The symbol "∿" means "is indifferent to."

64

and deciding for which π he is indifferent between choices. Axiom II obviously depends on the DM's ability, stipulated in Axiom I, to imagine a canonical lottery for c^* and c_* which yields c^* with canonical chance π for all possible π's. c^* and c_* correspond to W and L in the earlier discussion.

2.6 QUANTIFICATION OF LIKELIHOODS

Axiom III is the judgmental counterpart to Axiom II which stipulates the DM's ability to relate his feelings about the uncertain events upon which the outcome of his choice depends to canonical lotteries.

<u>Axiom III</u>. Let E be any event and let c^* and c_* be the consequences defined in Axiom II. The DM can quantify his judgment concerning E by specifying a number $p(E)$ between 0 and 1 inclusive such that he would be indifferent between a lottery which yields c^* if E occurs and c_* otherwise and a lottery which yields a canonical chance $p(E)$ at c^* and a complementary chance at c_*.

> Thus we relate the DM's judgmental feelings about the likelihood of E to canonical lotteries by asking him to consider the following set of choices and decide

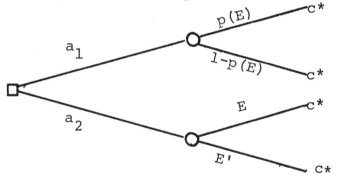

> for what canonical chance $p(E)$ he would be indifferent between the choices a_1 and a_2.

The three axioms stated so far allow us to measure the DM's feelings about consequences and uncertain events; however, by themselves they do not allow us to draw any inferences from these measurements. In order to do this, we must postulate two rules of behavior which the DM wishes his choices to follow. The first of these is transitivity.

2.7 TRANSITIVITY

<u>Axiom IV</u>   Let ℓ', ℓ'', and ℓ''' be three lotteries.
If the DM is indifferent between ℓ' and ℓ'' and is indifferent
between ℓ'' and ℓ''', then he is indifferent between ℓ' and ℓ'''.
If he is indifferent between ℓ' and ℓ'' but prefers ℓ'' to ℓ''',
then he prefers ℓ' to ℓ''', and so forth.

One argument for transitivity is that if your preferences violate it, you can be turned into a money pump.
Suppose a DM prefers lottery 1 to lottery 2, lottery 2
to lottery 3 and lottery 3 to lottery 1. That is, he
violates the axiom. Suppose such a DM starts out
with lottery 1. Well, if his preferences mean anything
at all, he would be willing to pay a slight premium to
exchange 1 for 3, say 25¢. He now has 3; hence, if
offered 2 for a slight premium, he would be willing
to exchange 3 for 2. He now has 2 and, since he prefers 1 to 2, he would be willing to pay a slight premium for 1, whereupon we offer this poor man 3 for a
slight premium, and so on. This DM's time to ruin is
solely a function of how fast he can make the ex-
changes. In general, unless one assumes some form of
transitivity, it is impossible to even think in terms
of rational decision-making for, by its very nature,
decision-making implies an ability to rank one's alternative outcomes and an intransitive ranking is no
ranking at all.

This is not to say that in real life people do not
exhibit intransitivity. We do so all the time. The
theory is not aimed at describing how people make decisions, but rather at indicating how they should make
decisions. Clearly, there would be no need for such
a normative theory if DM's always operated in a manner
consistent with the theory without ever having been
exposed to the theory itself.

2.8 SUBSTITUTABILITY

The second behavioral rule which we postulate is substitutability.

<u>Axiom V</u>. Let a lottery be modified by replacing one of
its consequences. If DM is indifferent between the replaced
consequence and its replacement, then he is indifferent between
the original and modified lotteries.

This is the "no fun in gambling" axiom. Since all
the other consequences in the lottery stay the same,

66

it would seem reasonable that the indifference between the replaced consequence and the replacement
would not change with the change in context. Once
again, however, in practice people violate this postulate. Each reader will have to decide for himself
whether or not he wants his decisions to obey this and
the preceding axiom. It might be a good idea at
this time if the reader went back and reviewed each
of the five axioms and see if there are any that he
can't stomach. Be warned, however, that if the answer is No, you have built yourself a straightjacket--
a rather comfortable straightjacket which will allow
you to analyze any problem, however complex, in an
internally consistent manner.

2.9 PROOF THAT p(E)'s ARE PROBABILITIES

Given these axioms, we now propose the following method of
attacking the core problem whose decision tree is shown on
page 2-20.

1) For each consequence, c, substitute the canonical
   lottery which gives a chance $\pi(c)$ at c* and a complementary chance at c_* .

2) Assign p(E) to each event branch resulting from the
   possible choices.

3) Reduce each of the resulting compound lotteries to a
   simple canonical lottery in c* and c_* taking expectations of the π-values.

4) Choose that alternative which reduces to the simple
   canonical lottery with the highest chance of yielding
   c*.

In order to justify this procedure, we will have to prove
two basic theorems. The first is:

Theorem I. The function p defined by Axiom III is a probability measure on the space of events $\{E_i\}$.

We will prove this and the following theorems by
making equivalence arguments between certain well-
chosen lotteries involving both real-world events
and the outcomes of a canonical experiment. In so
doing we will represent the lotteries both in the
now familiar decision tree form and by the following
somewhat more concise notation. Let $\{\gamma\}$ be a mutually exclusive and collectively exhaustive set of
outcomes of a canonical experiment and let $\{E_i\}$ be

67

mutually exclusive and collectively exhaustive set
of real-world events. One way of representing the
lottery which yields consequence c_{ji} if both E_i and γ
occur is by the array:

	E_1	E_2 .... E_i
γ_1	c_{11}	c_{12} ......
γ_2		
γ_j		c_{ji}
λ_N	c_{N1}	c_{NM}

We will use this notation often below.

The proof that all p(E)'s are non-negative--obey the first
axiom of probability--is direct from Axiom III. The proof that
p(E) and p(E') add to 1.00 is a little more interesting.

Using the above array notation, consider the following
lottery, ℓ, where the event E is a real-world event of interest
and the event γ is determined by a canonical lottery and has
canonical chance 1/2. Such a lottery exists by Axiom I.

	E	E'
γ	c^*	c_*
γ'	c_*	c^*

In tree form this lottery can be represented by

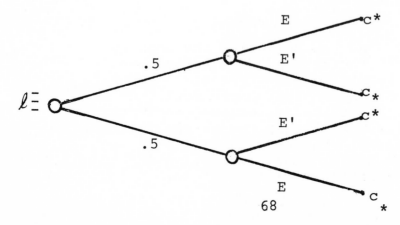

By Axiom III, there exists p(E) and p(E') such that

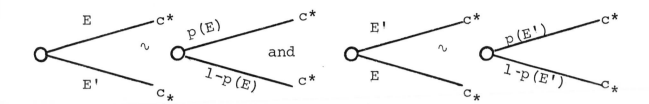

By Axiom V, we can substitute these indifferences into ℓ and obtain

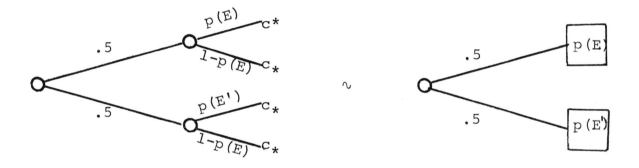

But the .5's, p(E) and p(E') are all canonical chances, thus probabilities. Applying the Sum Rule to the above lottery it can be reduced to

$$\boxed{\frac{p(E)+p(E')}{2}}$$

That is the lottery ℓ is equivalent to a $.5 \cdot (p(E)+p(E'))$-BRLT.

69

On the other hand an alternate representation of ℓ is

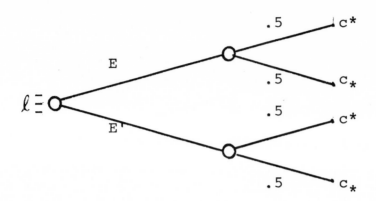

But by Axiom II both secondary lotteries are indifferent to $\boxed{.5}$.
Thus, by Axiom V

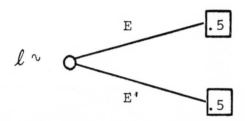

which lottery is equivalent to a .5-BRLT. Finally, using
transitivity, we have

$$\boxed{\frac{p(E)+p(E')}{2}} \quad \sim \quad \boxed{.5}$$

which by Axiom I implies

$$\frac{p(E)+p(E')}{2} = \frac{1}{2}$$

or the p's of an event and its complement sum to 1.0 which is
equivalent to saying that the p of the universal event is 1.0.

Finally, we must prove that, if E_1 and E_2 are mutually exclusive, then $p(E_1+E_2)=p(E_1)+p(E_2)$. Let E_3 be the complement of (E_1+E_2) and consider the following two lotteries where, as before, γ is an event having canonical chance .5.

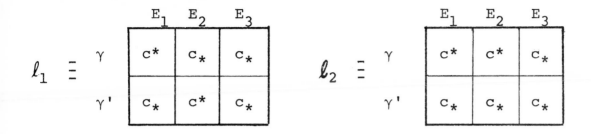

ℓ_1 and ℓ_2 may be represented as shown below.

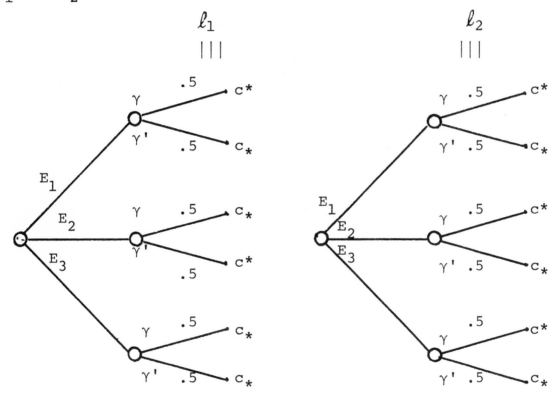

But in both cases middle branch is equivalent to a .5-BRLT. Therefore, by Axioms V and I, $\ell_1 \sim \ell_2$.

On the other hand, ℓ_1 and ℓ_2 may be represented as shown below.

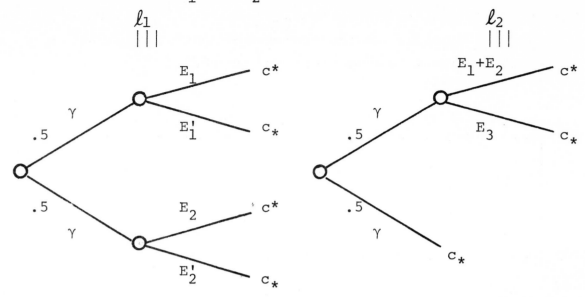

In ℓ_1, the upper arm is indifferent to $\boxed{p(E_1)}$ and the lower arm is indifferent to $\boxed{p(E_2)}$ by Axiom III. Thus, by substitutability, ℓ_1 is indifferent to

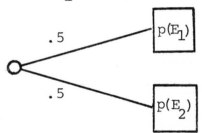

which, via the Sum Rule (which we can use since now we are dealing entirely with canonical chances which we have already proven are probabilities), is indifferent to

$$\boxed{\dfrac{p(E_1)+p(E_2)}{2}}$$

Again by Axiom III, the upper arm of ℓ_2 is indifferent to $\boxed{p(E_1+E_2)}$ and the lower arm to $\boxed{0}$. Thus, by substitution,

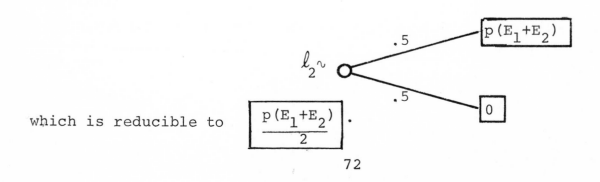

which is reducible to $\boxed{\dfrac{p(E_1+E_2)}{2}}$.

72

Since $\ell_1 \sim \ell_2$, by transitivity

$$\frac{P(E_1) + p(E_2)}{2} \sim \frac{P(E_1 + E_2)}{2}$$

which implies by Axiom I that

$$\frac{P(E_1) + p(E_2)}{2} = \frac{p(E_1 + E_2)}{2}$$

2.10   THE BASIC THEOREM

We are now in a position to prove our basic result--that any real lottery can be reduced to a basic reference lottery in the manner proposed earlier. To simplify notation, we will prove the theorem for the case where the real lottery has three possible outcomes. The extension to a larger number of outcomes is straightforward.

<u>Theorem II</u>.   Let E_1, E_2 and E_3 be three mutually exclusive and exhaustive events, then the lottery yielding c_1 if E_1 occurs, c_2 if E_2 occurs and c_3 if E_3 occurs is indifferent to the lottery, ℓ, yielding a π chance at c^* and a complementary chance at c_* where

$$\pi = \sum_i p(E_i) \pi(c_i)$$

By Axioms I, II, and V we replace the consequences in ℓ by canonical lotteries on c^* and c_*. Thus,

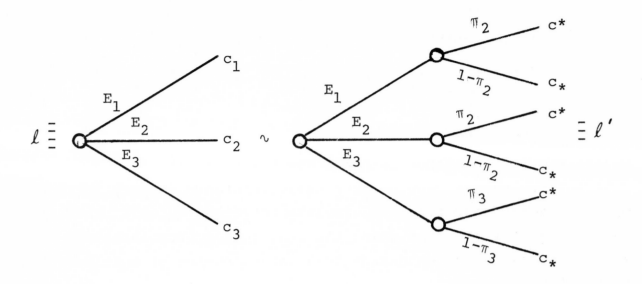

Assume without loss of generality that the c_i have been ordered such that $\pi_1 > \pi_2 > \pi_3$. By Axiom I, we can construct a canonical experiment with four possible outcomes, $(\gamma_1, \gamma_2, \gamma_3, \gamma_4)$ such that

γ_1 has canonical chance π_3

γ_2 has canonical chance $(\pi_2 - \pi_3)$

γ_3 has canonical chance $(\pi_1 - \pi_2)$

γ_4 has canonical chance $(1 - \pi_1)$

Now consider the following compound lottery:

	E_1	E_2'	E_3	
γ_1	c^*	c^*	c^*	
γ_2	c^*	c^*	c_*	$\equiv \ell''$
γ_3	c^*	c_*	c_*	
γ_4	c_*	c_*	c_*	

74

The reader can verify that, for each E_i, this compound lottery yields the canonical chance at c* called for by lottery ℓ'. Thus $\ell'' \sim \ell'$. But ℓ'' can be represented by

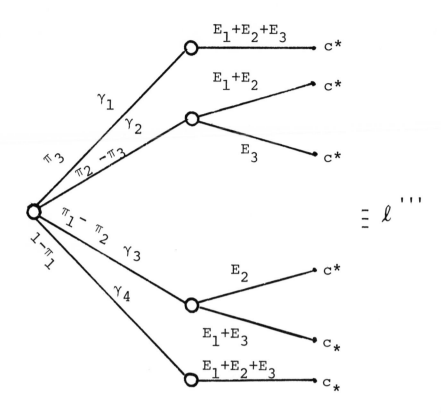

But by Axioms III and V and the fact that the function, $p(E_i)$ is a probability, this lottery is indifferent to

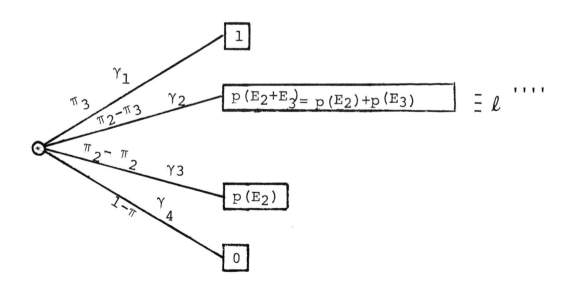

But now we have everything in terms of canonical chances on
c and c_* which are probabilities. Therefore, using the
Sum Rule, we find that the above lottery reduces to a
$p_1 \cdot \pi_1 + p_2 \cdot \pi_2 + p_3 \cdot \pi_3$ canonical chance at c^* and a complementary chance at c_ℓ.

$$\ell \sim \boxed{p_1 \; \pi_1 + p_2 \; \pi_2 + p_3 \pi_3}$$

2.11 DEFINITION OF CONDITIONAL PROBABILITY AND JUSTIFICATION
OF BAYES RULE

We already have all the basics of Bayesian decision theory.
However, we need one more definition and proof in order to in-
struct a DM who is willing to accept the axioms as to how he
should change his subjective probabilities as new information
becomes available.

Consider the following lottery where E_1 and E_2 are real-
world events such that $E_1 + E_2 = U$ and γ is an event determined by
a canonical experiment.

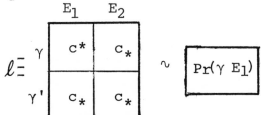

Def.: <u>Given that</u> γ <u>occurs</u>, the canonical chance, p, such that
DM is indifferent between a lottery offering c^* if E_1 occurs
and c_* otherwise and a canonical lottery offering c^* with
chance p and c_* with chance 1-p is called the <u>conditional</u>
<u>probability</u> of E_1 given γ and denoted $Pr(E_1|\gamma)$. There is an analo-
gous definition for $Pr(\gamma|E_1)$.

THEOREM: Justification of Bayes Rule for subjective conditional
probability.

ℓ above has two representations

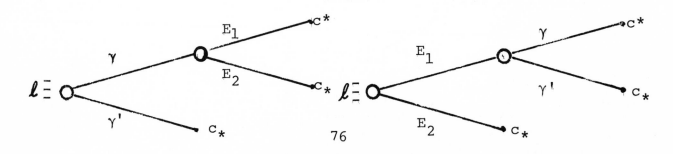

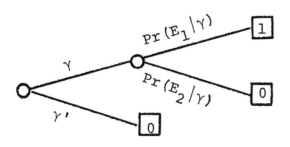

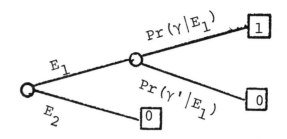

By Sum Rule since we are
dealing with canonical
chances

$$\boxed{\Pr(\gamma) \cdot \Pr(E_1 | \gamma)}$$

By Sum Rule

$$\boxed{\Pr(E_1) \Pr(\gamma | E_1)}$$

By Transitivity & Axiom I

$$\Pr(\gamma \cdot E_1) = \Pr(\gamma) \Pr(E_1 | \gamma)$$

By Transitivity & Axiom I

$$\Pr(\gamma \cdot E_1) = \Pr(\gamma | E_1) \Pr(E_1)$$

Interchanging roles of E_1 and E_2, we also have $\Pr(\gamma \cdot E_2) = \Pr(\gamma | E_2) \Pr(E_2) = \Pr(\gamma) \Pr(E_2 | \gamma)$.

Since $\Pr(\gamma)$ is a probability, the Sum Rule holds and

$$\Pr(\gamma) = \Pr(\gamma E_1) + \Pr(\gamma E_2)$$

or

$$\Pr(\gamma) = \Pr(\gamma | E_1) \Pr(E_1) + \Pr(\gamma | E_2) \Pr(E_2)$$

Combining

$$\Pr(E_1 | \gamma) = \frac{\Pr(\gamma | E_1) \Pr(E_1)}{\Pr(\gamma | E_1) \Pr(E_1) + \Pr(\gamma | E_2) \Pr(E_2)}$$

which proves Bayes Rule.

What we have shown is that using this definition of conditional probability which is based on the DM's indifferences, then the DM who accepts the postulates of decision theory should update his subjective likelihoods according to Bayes Rule. This then is the justification of our approach to Joe's problem of evaluating his test results.

2.12 SOME EMPIRICAL DATA

Well, we have come to the end of our purely deductive reasoning about the five basic postulates of decision theory-- no doubt with some relief. A natural question is: has it ever been tried? There have been several attempts to assess real-world decision-makers' preference functions and to determine to what degree their decisions are consistent with these functions. Most of this work has been aimed at inland oil and gas operators, e.g., references 5 and 6. These studies showed that it was possible to get DMs to display consistent preference functions, which they were willing to stick with, that the DMs interviewed displayed a rather large spectrum of attitudes toward risk, ranging from very risk-adverse (such as our friend Joe) through close to EMV'er to, in some cases, willingness to take negative expected value bets in certain situations. In references 5 and 6 no examination of the degree to which these DMs' actual decisions were consistent with their preferences was undertaken. More recently, Lorange and Norman, references 10 and 11, interviewed 17 Scandinavian shipowners. Fourteen of the owners had no difficulty answering the type of questions posed on pages 50 and 52 and only two had major difficulty comparing the hypothetical lotteries offered. These authors used a W of -$15 million and a L of -$1.5 million. Most of their questions were phrased in terms of 50-50 gambles. In situations where the owners were told to assume that their borrowing powers would be unaffected by their asset position, all but two of the owners were risk-prone, that is, they would be willing to accept negative expected value bets over a significant range of the outcomes. When told to assume that the company could sustain a loss of 1.5 million dollars but not much more without affecting borrowing power, only about half the owners became risk-adverse. This is a highly unusual set of results and certainly lends credence to the conventional wisdom that shipowners, or at least Scandinavian shipowners, are unusually willing to take risks.* Lorange and Norman went further and studied the actual behavior of these owners. They found that, on the whole, those owners who displayed highly risk-prone preference functions had fleets with a high percentage of tankers. They also found that the more risk-prone owners had significantly shorter average charter contracts than their more risk-adverse colleagues. In short, in a very general and loose sense, the owners seemed to be operating in a manner that was consistent with their preference functions in that the risk-prone owners tended to devote more of their capital to the high-risk trades.

As a postscript, the owners displayed considerable interest in the interview and its results. It is, of course, doubtful whether they took their preference functions back to the office and put them to use. However, the following chapters will indicate how they might do so, if they so choose, i.e., if they had decided to accept the five basic postulates of decision-making under uncertainty.

---

*It should be noted that even if a DM were willing to take a negative expected value bet, he would not do so until he had exhausted all positive expected value bets over the same range. Since an investor can usually find a positive expected value bet somewhere, acceptance of negative expected value gambles is probably best explained by a desire to stay in this particular business.

CHAPTER 3

SEQUENCES OF DECISIONS AND DYNAMIC PROGRAMMING

Well, we have a method which in principle can handle any problem. However, as the example of Joe's problem indicates, it doesn't take very long before even the simplest decision tree grows into a messy bush. Joe had only two decisions: which test to use and whether to buy, buy with guarantee or refuse the ship after the chosen test was over. Joe had essentially a two-stage problem. Yet with only two stages the tree had already grown too big to fit on a single page.

Typically, real-world problems will involve a large number of stages. An offshore oil operator contemplating opening up a new field faces a set of exploration and development decisions involving at least ten separate stages. A shipowner operating in the charter market will make a decision on the average of about once every two months with respect to the employment of his ship--a sequence of decisions which will involve over 100 separate stages during the life of the ship. In general, the number of possible paths in a decision tree is of the order of M^N where M is the number of options open to the shipowner at any point in the sequence and N is the number of stages in the sequence.* Clearly, our brute force method of folding back the entire tree quickly becomes unworkable as N becomes even moderately large.

In Joe's original problem, we were able to take advantage of the structure of the tree in order to save us some work. We found that we were able to evaluate test plan T_3 by relating various nodes of this plan to nodes we had already evaluated under test plans T_1 and T_2. With this as a hint, let us turn to a very simple sequential problem under certainty and see if we can't formalize a method for taking advantage of the fact that often there are a variety of paths which lead to essentially the same point in a decision tree.

---

*Actually, the tree is much larger even than this when the chance nodes are accounted for.

3.1 THE CONCEPT OF DYNAMIC PROGRAMMING

Consider the following completely deterministic problem. We have the network shown in Figure 3-1. We wish to traverse this network from A to Z. This might be a traffic light network or an extremely simple and regular production process network. In any event, associated with each link is a cost (money or time). These costs are the numbers shown on each link. Our problem is to find that path from A to Z which minimizes the traversal cost.

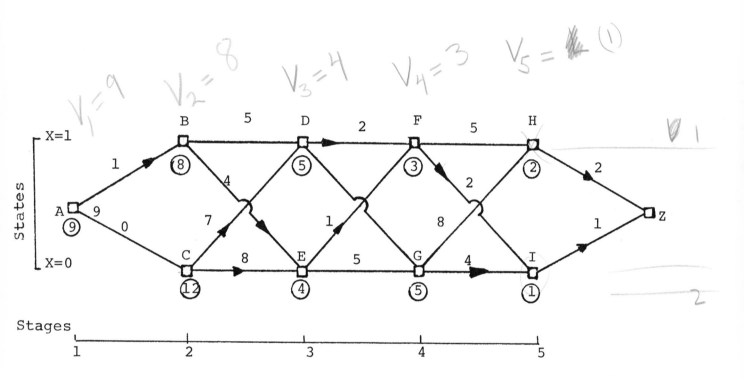

One obvious possibility is simply to enumerate all the possible paths and pick the one with the lowest cost. There are $2^4=16$ paths, so this is no great undertaking. However, being of an especially lazy and contrary nature, we decide that this is both too time-consuming and too straightforward. We ask ourselves: Is there a way that we can make use of the regular structure of the problem to reduce our computational travail?

The first thing we note is that the problem, like many much more complicated problems, is a sequential one. We may imagine that we construct our path by first choosing a branch from A. We call this choice the first *stage* of the process. At the second stage, we choose a branch leading from the terminal node of our first choice, and so on. To make the second choice we need to know which of the two nodes B or C is the terminal node of our first choice. We call the designation of this terminal node the *state* of the system at stage 2. Similarly, at stage 2 we can pick a branch if we know at which of D and C we are. From this viewpoint we have five individual decisions and a five-stage decision process.

Given this structure, how shall we generate the sequence of decisions which produces the path of minimum cost? We reason as follows. Suppose we somehow knew the value of the minimum cost path associated with each of the following two shorter problems:

1) The path connecting B and Z;
2) The path connecting C and Z.

Then we could easily evaluate the particular path from A to Z which has AB as its initial branch and whose four remaining branches constitute the path of minimum cost from B to Z by simply adding the cost of branch AB to the cost of the minimum cost path from B to Z. Any other path from A to Z with AB as its first branch will be inferior to this one. Similarly, one can calculate the minimum cost of the path from A to Z with AC as its first arc by adding the cost of AC to the cost of the minimum cost path from C to Z. These are the only two possibilities. So it is clear that we would have no trouble determining the best initial branch if we knew the values of the minimum cost paths from both B and C to Z. *Note that as far as the first stage decision is concerned, it is not the identification of the minimum cost paths from B and C to Z, but the values of these paths which is the vital information.*

82

Continuing this line of reasoning, we could easily determine the values of the minimum cost paths from both B and C to Z if we somehow knew the values of the minimum cost paths from both D and E to Z. Just as we reasoned earlier that we could solve the original five-state problem if we had already solved two four-stage problems, we can now relate each of the four-stage problems to two three-stage problems; that is, the determination of the minimum value paths from both D and E to Z. This recursive reasoning can be continued until we need only the values of the minimum value path from each of H and I to Z. But these values are easily obtained, since there are no free choices associated with each of these last two problems. The values of the minimum cost paths from H and I to Z are 2 and 1 respectively. These values we associated with the nodes H and I. In the figure we have placed these values in circles under their respective nodes.

We can now move back to each of the decisions at stage 4. If we are at F we have the choice of going to H at a cost of 5 and we know from the circled quantity at H that the minimum cost path from H on has a value of 2. Thus, the value of the alternative is 5 + 2 or 7. On the other hand, if we choose to proceed to I at a cost of 2 we know from the circled quantity at I that the minimum cost path from I on has a value of 1 for a total cost of 3. 3 is better than 7; so the indicated action if we are at F is to go to I. We have shown an arrow indicating this choice and have placed its value, 3, in the circle under F. Similarly, if we are at G we would determine that the minimum cost path is towards I and has a value of 5.

We can now proceed in a similar manner to the two three-stage problems starting at D and E and determine that the respective values associated with these nodes are 5 and 4 with the arrows designating the minimizing direction. Notice that, in solving the two problems emanating from D and E, only the values assigned to the next stage, those at F and G, are relevant. This has important implications for much larger problems in which computer memory constraints are a consideration.

83

In order to calculate the values for stage n we need only the answers for stage n+1.

Proceeding in a similar manner to the two four-stage problems and finally to the five-stage problem yields the circled values and arrows shown in the figure. The value of the minimum cost path is 9, and it is an extremely simple manner to determine that path by simply following the arrows, starting at A. It is ABEFIZ. Indeed, one need not and in general one doesn't bother to keep track of the arrows for one can always tell the cost minimizing decision for any particular node from the circled quantities.

Suppose we had forgotten to draw the arrow emanating from E as we moved backward calculating the value of the cost minimizing paths. After completing this calculation and then moving forward from A to E, we would have no direct guidance about which way to go. However, we could easily figure out which way to go by repeating our original computation at E. If we go to G, the best we can do is 5+4 or 9 while if we go to F the best we can do is 1+3 or 4. F is the obvious choice, and , of course, the value of this choice must equal the circled quantity at E. Clearly, by such reasoning we could do away with all the arrows if we so chose. The value of the circled quantities by themselves determines the minimizing path. In bigger problems, we will sometimes make use of this fact to decrease computer memory requirements.

In summary, once one has the value of the minimal cost path for all nodes, then one has the minimizing path. Notice also that we have solved somewhat more than our original problem. We have solved the problem of finding the minimizing path from any node to Z.* In this case, this additional information was not needed. We shall see that when we move to decisions under uncertainty this information which, if you like, comes

---

* Notice that for node C we have the interesting but not troublesome case of both choices being cost-minimizing. If we are at C, it doesn't make any difference which link we choose.

free is of considerable interest.

We have outlined a rather roundabout way of solving a very simple problem. We may well ask ourselves: What are its computational advantages? Compared with direct enumeration, at least, they are considerable. Using direct enumeration, we have 2^4 paths and the evaluation of each path requires 4 + 1 additions. Thus, total additions by enumeration = $(4+1) \cdot 2^4 = 80$. By our backwards recursion method, we must solve $2 \cdot 4 + 1$ two-stage problems, each involving two additions for a total of $2 \cdot (2 \cdot 4 + 1) = 18$.* Eighteen additions versus 80 is not a considerable matter in these days of microsecond computers, but consider what would happen if we had, as in a real problem, 100 stages. Then direct enumeration leads to $(101) \cdot 2^{100} \approx 10^{30}$ additions, while backwards recursion requires only $2 \cdot (2 \cdot 100 + 1) = 402$ additions. Matters get still worse if, instead of two alternatives at each node, there are 10 possible links leading from each node to 10 possible nodes at the next stage--still a small number of alternatives by real-world standards. In this case direct enumeration leads to $(101) \cdot 10^{100}$ additions, while backwards recursion requires $10 \cdot (10 \cdot 100 + 1) = 10,010$ additions. With direct enumeration the number of computations increases exponentially with both the number of stages and the number of alternatives at each stage. With backwards recursion, computation increases linearly with the number of stages and as the square of the number of alternatives at each stage. The relative efficiency of the latter is obvious.

In view of this relative efficiency, we now proceed to formalize the method we have outlined, which is called _dynamic programming_.

3.2   THE OPTIMAL VALUE FUNCTION

We start off with some definitions:

The _stage_ of the process is the position within the sequence

---

* Since direct enumeration is a strawman, I am ignoring the number of comparisons which also work out to the advantage of the recursive approach.

of decisions of the decision presently being considered.

The *state* of the system at any stage is the information
necessary to render the decision at that stage.

Let n denote the present stage and x denote the present
state. Then over all possible combinations of stage and state
we define a function, $V_n(x)$, called the *optimal value function*
to be the extremal value (minimum or maximum) of the DM's objective associated with being in state x at stage n. It is the
best he can do from this state and stage to the end of the
process.

In order to define an optimal value function for our little
network problem we need to have a method for denoting the state
at any stage. In this case there are only two possible states
and a possible representation is x=1 if we are on the upper
branch of the network and x=0 if we are on the lower branch.
The optimal value function $V_n(x)$ then is the value of the minimum cost path from the node corresponding to the pair (n,x) on.
Using our earlier reasoning we see that this function obeys the
following equation.

$$V_n(x) = \min \begin{cases} c_u(n,x) + V_{n+1}(1) \\ \\ c_d(n,x) + V_{n+1}(0) \end{cases}$$

for n=1,2,3,4 and x=0 and 1. In this equation $c_u(n,x)$ denotes
the cost associated with the upper link emanating from the node
(n,x) and $c_d(n,x)$ is the cost of the lower link from that node.
For n=5, the equation becomes even simpler:

$$V_5(1) = 2; \quad V_5(0) = 1$$

This is the boundary condition at the end of the decision
process. Our backward-thinking computational procedure involves
substituting this boundary condition into the right-hand side
of the above relation, solving for $V_4(1)$ and $V_4(0)$ using this
relation, and then substituting the results of this computa-

tion into the same r.h.s. of the equation, solving for V_3, and so on. Having calculated the optimal value function for all combinations of stage and state by this backwards process we are ready to determine the cost-minimizing set of choices. To do this we begin at the beginning for a change and see which of the two expressions, $c_u(0,0)+V_2(1)$ or $c_d(0,0)+V_2(0)$, equals $V_1(0)$. The branch corresponding to equality is the cost-minimizing choice at stage 1. We move along that branch to the next stage and then repeat the process of comparing the optimal value of the stage and state we are at to the value derived from summing the cost of each possible link and the optimal values of the stage and state to which each of these links lead. In this manner, we can work our way forward through the network determining the optimal set of choices. If we had bothered to store all the cost-minimizing choices during the backwards recursion, we could avoid this step and simply move forward through the network following these choices. In real problems, memory is usually tighter than time, so we generally take the more roundabout method.

3.3 AN INVENTORY PROBLEM

We now want to apply our newly-learned technique, dynamic programming to a somewhat more realistic problem. Let us suppose that we are a shipyard contemplating the problem of what should be the timing and magnitude of orders for some fairly specialized piece of equipment which is used in all or most of the ships we produce--say, some seagoing valve. The considerations are as follows. The manufacturer of the valve prefers large orders due to savings in transaction and setup costs and sets his price to reflect these economies. Let us take an extreme example and assume that the price as a function of order quantity is of the form

$$C(y) = \$100 + \$150 \cdot y$$

Here, y is the number of valves ordered. We also know from our production schedule what the need for these valves will be in each month over the time interval being considered, say, a year.

We assume it is given by the following table.

Month	1	2	3	4	5	6	7	8	9	10	11	12
Valves	8	1	2	9	12	0	4	7	2	10	1	6

If we ordered all 62 valves at the beginning of the year, we would pay the setput charge only once. However, our accountants tell us that warehousing, maintenance and financing costs of carrying a valve in inventory for a month are $1.00. The problem then is: how many valves should we order when to minimize valve expenses, given that we are going to meet the production line needs. Bloated by our earlier stunning success on the little network problem, we decide to use dynamic programming. Dynamic programming involves four basic steps:

1) Is the problem a sequential one and, if so, what are the stages? In this case, it is pretty clear that the problem is a sequential one, the individual decisions in the sequences being the choice of the number of valves to be ordered at the beginning of each month. We have 12 stages: $n=1,2,\ldots,12$.

2) What is the state of the system at each stage? What do we need to know in order to make the individual decision at the beginning of each month? Answer: we need to know the present level of our stock of valves. Let us denote this level, the state, at the beginning of month n by x_n.

3) Define the optimal value function. For this problem, $V_n(x_n)$ is the minimum cost of buying and storing valves for the remainder of the year, given that we are at the beginning of the nth month and we presently have x_n valves on hand.

4) Derive the equation relating the values of the optimal value function at stage n to the values of this function at stage n+1. This derivation involves three substeps:

   a) What are the alternatives at n, given that we have

88

x_n valves? In this problem, we can order any number of valves from 0 to $D_n - x_n$ where D_n is the cumulative demand for valves from n on. (Given our problem statement there is never any point in ordering more than $D_n - x_n$ valves.) However, if the need in the present month, d_n, is greater than x_n, then we must order at least $d_n - x_n$.

b) What does a particular alternative do to the value of the state variable, x_{n+1}? What state will it get us into at time n+1? Let y_n be the number of valves ordered at n, possibly 0, then $x_{n+1} = x_n - d_n + y_n$.

c) How does a particular individual alternative affect the costs incurred in the period between the decision at n and the decision at n+1, given we are at n and have x_n available? In this case, if we order $y_n > 0$ then we must pay $100 + 150y_n$; if $y_n = 0$ then we pay out nothing. In addition, through the ensuing month we will be carrying $x_n - d_n + y_n$ valves in inventory at a unit cost of $1.00.

Putting this all together, we see that the required relation linking V_n and V_{n+1} is

$$V_n(x_n) = \operatorname*{minimum}_{\underline{y}_n \leq Y_n \leq \bar{y}_n} \quad 1.00 \cdot (x_n - d_n + y_n) + \left\{ \begin{array}{l} 0 \text{ if } y_n = 0 \\ \\ 100 + 150y_n \text{ if } y_n > 0 \end{array} \right\}$$
$$+ \quad V_{n+1}(x_n - d_n + y_n)$$

where the lower limit on $y_n, \underline{y}_n$, is equal to max $(0, d_n - x_n)$ and the upper limit, $\bar{y}_n$, is equal to $D_n - x_n$ where $D_n = \sum_{k=n}^{12} d_n$.

This relation holds for all n=1,2,...,12 and for all $x_n = 0, 1, ..., D_n$. The boundary condition at the end of the process, given that we are going to ignore costs incurred after the end of the year, can be most simply represented by setting $V_{13}(x_{13})$

equal to zero for all x_{13}. The procedure then is to plug this boundary condition into the right-hand side of the above relation and solve for V_{12} for all x_{12}. V_{12} in turn is substituted into the relation and we solve for V_{11}, and continuing in this manner we work our way backwards to the first stage. At that point we will have computed the complete optimal value function table. It is now a simple matter to work our way forward through the optimal value function tables picking out the cost-minimizing alternatives as we did in the network problem.

Perhaps it will help our understanding of dynamic programing, and it will certainly indicate the ease with which one can implement dynamic programming on the computer, if we display a computer program which accomplishes this set of computations. Such a program is shown in Figure 3-2. This particular program is written in PL/1, but Fortran programmers will have no problem following the logic. Readers unfamiliar with a high level compiler can skip to the next section without any loss in logical continuity.

The core of the program, the calculation of the optimal value table consists of three loops: a loop over the stage variable N, which runs from large N to small, a loop over the state variable X, and within these two loops a loop to determine the cost-minimizing Y for the particular combination of stage and state.* After the optimal value function table, V(N,X), is calculated, a single loop, moving forward over the stage variable, suffices to pick out the cost-minimizing strategy. If core memory space were a problem, we would not store the cost minimizing choice for each stage and state, but rather compute the cost minimizing sequence of decisions directly from the optimal value function table in which case the second part of

_____

*Obviously, blindly trying all possible alternatives at each combination of stage and state, as this program does, is grossly inefficient. In the sequel, we will often go to considerable pains to make sure this inner extremization is accomplished as efficiently as possible, since it has to be done a large number of times.

```
/*THIS PROCEDURE CALCULATES OPTIMAL VALVE ORDERING POLICY VIA D.P.   */
/*N=STAGE. NMAX=MAX NO OF STAGES (24 OR LESS IN THIS PROGRAM).        */
/*X=STATE. XMAX=MAX NO OF STATES (100 OR LESS IN THIS PROGRAM).       */
/*V(N,X)=OPTIMAL VALUE TABLE. Y(N,X)=OPTIMAL POLICY TABLE.            */
/*D(N)=NO OF VALVES DEMANDED AT STAGE N.                             */
/*DSUM(N)=CUMULATIVE NO OF VALVES DEMANDED IN STAGES N THRU NMAX.     */

DYNAMIC_PROGRAM:PROCEDURE OPTIONS(MAIN);
             DECLARE V(25,0:100),Y(25,0:100) FIXED,
                      (N,NMAX,X,XMAX,YTRIAL,D(24),DSUM(24)) FIXED;
             GET LIST (NMAX,XMAX,D,DSUM);

/*SET BOUNDARY CONDITIONS AT N=NMAX+1.                               */
          DO X=0 TO XMAX;
              V(NMAX+1,X)=0.0;
          END;

z*CALCULATE OPTIMAL VALUE FUNCTION BY BACKWARDS RECURSION.           */
STAGE_LOOP: DO N=NMAX TO 1 BY -1;
STATE_LOOP:          DO X=0 TO XMAX;
                        V(N,X)=999999.9;
CHOICE_LOOP:              DO YTRIAL=MAX(0,D(N)-X) TO DSUM(N) X;
                            IF YTRIAL=0 THEN ORDER_COST=0.0;
                                    ELSE ORDER_COST=100+100*YTRIAL;
                            STORAGE_COST=1.00*(X-D(N)+YTRIAL);
                            VTRIAL=ORDER_COST+STORAGE_COST
                                        +V(N+1,X-D(N)+YTRIAL);
                            IF VTRIAL<V(N,X) THEN DO;
                                            V(N,X)=VTRIAL;
                                            Y(N,X)=YTRIAL;
                                         END;
                        END CHOICE LOOP;
                    END STATE-LOOP;
          END STAGE_LOOP;
/*DETERMINE COST MINIMIZING SEQUENCE OF DECISIONS BY MOVING           */
/*FORWARD THRU OPTIMAL POLICY TABLE.                                 */
        X=0;
        DO N=1 TO NMAX;
            PUT SKIP EDIT ('OPTIMAL CHOICE AT STAGE',N,'IS TO ORDER',
                         Y(N,X),'VALVES.') (A(22),F(4),A(11),F(4),
                                          A(7));
            X=X-D(N)+Y(N,X);
        END;
END DYNAMIC_PROGRAM;
```

FIGURE 3-2

the program would look like.

```
/*DETERMINE COST MINIMIZING SEQUENCE OF DECISIONS BY MOVING FORWARD */
/*THRU OPTIMAL VALUE FUNCTION TABLE.                               */
        X=0;
        DO N=1 TO NMAX;
            DO YTRIAL=MAX(0,D(N)-X) TO DSUM(N)-X;
                IF YTRIAL=0 THEN ORDER_COST=0.0;
                            ELSE ORDER_COST=100+100*YTRIAL:
                STORAGE_COST=1.00*(X-D(N)+YTRIAL);
                VTRIAL=ORDER_COST+STORAGE_COST+V(N+1,X-D(N)+YTRIAL);
                IF VTRIAL=V(N,X) THEN GO TO FOUND_Y;
            END;
FOUND_Y:PUT SKIP EDIT ('OPTIMAL CHOICE AT STAGE',N,'IS TO ORDER',
                YTRIAL,'VALVES.') (A(22),F(4),A(11),F(4),A(7));
        X=X-D(N)+YTRIAL;
        END;
END DYNAMIC_PROGRAM;
```

Further, there is no need to keep the complete optimal value function table in core memory. If desired, after using $V(N+1,X)$ to compute $V(N,X)$ we can dispatch $V(N+1,X)$ to tape or disk to be recalled at the proper time during the search forward through the table to determine the cost-minimizing sequence. Thus, at any particular time we need devote no more than $2 \cdot XMAX$ words of core storage to the storage of the optimal value function tables.

In any event, in solving this problem our computational effort will be proportional to the number of stages (12), times the number of possible states at each stage (always less than 63), times the number of operations required in order to compute the recursion relations for each stage-state combination (certainly less than 200). Therefore, the number of computer operations required to solve this problem by dynamic programming is less than 12x63x100=75,600 which is a trivial number by modern computer's standards. The number of conceivable policies for this problem is of the order of 30^{12} or about 5.3×10^{16}.

3.4 A SHIP PRODUCTION SCHEDULING PROBLEM

We now want to turn to a slightly larger-scale problem which will bring out some other facets of dynamic programming and also point out some of its limitations. This problem arose in a submarine yard where it takes on its most virulent form. However, the same problem exists in all conventional ship construction. We will discuss it in the submarine context.

The labor force requirements of a submarine change radically while the submarine is under construction--each submarine demands a different mix of workers at different stages in its construction. Let us for simplicity say that there are only three trades relevant to submarine construction: welders, fitters, electricians. We can represent the varying requirements for each of these trades during the ship's construction by Figure 3-3 which under the assumption that percentage completion is proportional to man-hours applied plots the number of man-hours of each trade required to effect 1% completion as a function of how far along in the construction process the submarine is.

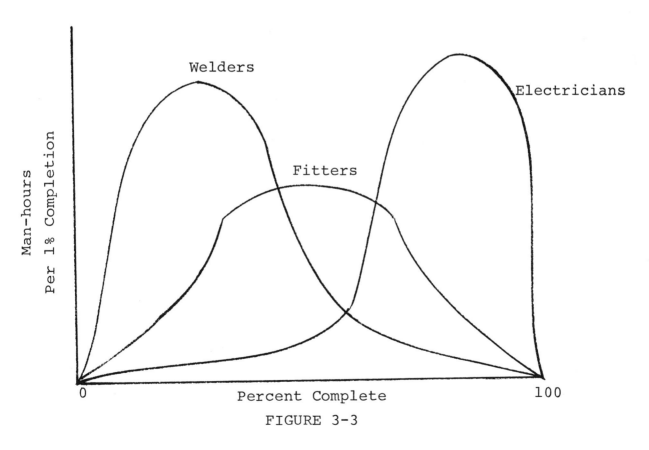

FIGURE 3-3

These variations give rise to variations in the total amount of a particular trade demanded at any given time, even if the yard is booked to full capacity. The submarine yard in question noted that at times certain trades would be working considerable amounts of overtime and other trades would be laying off or underemployed. The personnel people were completely confused by the situation and had no idea what constituted a rational labor force policy. Since the periods of the oscillation were of the order of months, in some circles they were attributed to seasonal factors.

The yard kept track of the completion histories of all past jobs. They were as displayed in Figure 3-4.

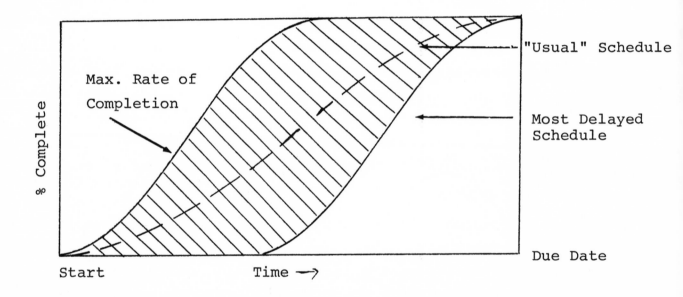

FIGURE 3.4 POSSIBLE PRODUCTION SCHEDULES

Any nondecreasing curve in the shaded area whose slope is everywhere less than the maximum slope in a feasible construction schedule. The general policy then in effect was to advance the construction of each submarine at an average rate with the exception that , if a submarine got behind schedule, extra effort was shifted to that submarine in order to insure its completion by the deadline. It should be clear that considerable flexibility existed with respect to construction rates. The question then became: Would it be possible to juggle the construction schedules of the various submarines in such a way as to smooth out the variations in the demands on the various trades?

For reasons which will become clear, the problem of determining that coupled labor force/production schedule policy which minimizes the total labor costs of constructing the submarines was judged to be computationally infeasible. Thus, the analyst responsible for developing the improved production schedules fell back on a subproblem. To wit, given specified levels of each trade T_i, i=1,2,3, where it is convenient to express the T_i's in terms of the regular man-hours of trade i available in a two-week period, determine that production schedule for each sub which collectively results in the lowest loss due to yardwide fluctuations in the level of demand for each trade. At the time that this analysis was done a reasonable measure of this loss seemed to be the sum of the cost of overtime plus the cost of undertime where undertime was defined to be excess in the number of regular-time man-hours available in a trade over the number of regular man-hours of that trade actually required by the production schedule.

Let us suppose further that we have three submarines to be constructed, each with given deadlines. We are going to review our construction progress periodically, say, every two weeks. Thus, the stages of the process become the review times. If we are scheduling construction over a three-year period, we would have some 75 stages. We describe the state of the system at any given time by the percentage completion of each of our submarines, (C_1, C_2, C_3). Note that in this problem the state must be described by a number of variables (a vector) rather than a single number. In reviewing the state of completion in percentage terms, we round off to the nearest even integer. Thus, at any particular stage we can have as many as $50^3 = 125,000$ states.

Given a particular combination of stage and state, what are our alternatives? We have control over the completion rate of each submarine for the next two weeks. Denote the completion rate ordered on submarine k by r_k. In general, r_k can be anywhere between 0 and the maximum rate for the present state of completion of the kth submarine unless we are on the upward sloping portion of the lower border of Figure 3-4, in which case we must proceed at the maximum completion rate in order to meet the deadline.

Given that we are at the nth review period with state (C_1,C_2,C_3) and we pick some completion rate r_k, k=1,2,3 for each submarine, what is the effect on the labor force? Let the man-hours of trade i per percent completion of submarine k as a function of state of completion be $m_i(C_k)$. The m_i's are the functions portrayed in Figure 3-3. Then the total number of man-hours of trade i required in the ensuing two-week period, given that the present state is (C_1,C_2,C_3) and we choose (r_1,r_2,r_3) rates of completion per two-week period, is

$$H_i(C_1,C_2,C_3;r_1,r_2,r_3) = \sum_{k=1}^{3} r_k \cdot m_i(C_k)$$

But the regular-time man-hours available during this period of this trade is T_i. Thus, the costs of overtime/undertime in this trade for the next two-week period, given this situation, will be

$$G_i(C_1,C_2,C_3;r_1,r_2 r_3) = \begin{cases} w_i \cdot [T_i - H_i(C_1,C_2,C_3;r_1,r_2,r_3)] & \text{if } T_i > H_i \\ w_i^* \cdot [H_i(C_1,C_2,C_3;r_1,r_2,r_3) - T_i] & \text{if } T_i > H_i \end{cases}$$

where w_i is the regular wage rate for the ith r trade and w_i* is the overtime rate for this trade. The total overtime/unemployment cost for the yard in the nth period is G_i summed over all trades, or

$$B_n(C_1,C_2,C_3;r_1,r_2,r_3) = \sum_{i=1}^{3} G_i(C_1,C_2,C_3;r_1,r_2,r_3)$$

The problem is to find that possible set of construction schedules which minimizes B_n summed over all periods.

Reasoning as before, we define $V_n(C_1,C_2,C_3)$ to be the minimum overtime/undertime cost attainable for the remainder of the period being scheduled, given that we are presently at the nth review period and the state of completion is characterized by (C_1,C_2,C_3). The recursion relation for V_n is

$$V_n(C_1,C_2,C_3) = \underset{\{r_1,r_2,r_3\}}{\text{minimum}} \left\{ \begin{array}{l} B_n(C_1,C_2,C_3;r_1,r_2,r_3) \\ \\ + V_{n+1}(C_1+r_1,C_2+r_2,C_3+r_3) \end{array} \right.$$

where the minimum is taken over all feasible r_k's.

This recursion relation holds for all n=1,2,...,N where N is the review corresponding to the last due date. No costs (given our problem statement) are incurred thereafter, so we can represent the boundary condition by $V_{N+1}(C_1,C_2,C_3)=0$ for all possible (C_1,C_2,C_3). We can now compute the optimal value function as before by backward recursion.

Now, however, this computation is no trivial task. We have some 75 stages, as many as 125,000 possible states at each stage, and the calculation at each stage and state will involve several hundred computer operations. Therefore, we are talking about some 40×10^8 operations, which even on a microsecond machine will require about an hour. More important, at any point we must store the values of the optimal value function for all possible states for that stage which we have just completed (n+1), as well as those for the stage we are presently working on (n). This will require 250,000 words of memory. Thus, this is about as large a problem as can usefully be tackled with present machines. Consider what would happen if we had four or five submarines. For four the number of states is 50^4, for five it is 50^5 or 312 million. In short, dynamic programming often breaks down in the face of multivariable state descriptions, for the number of possible states increases exponentially with the number of state variables.

The approach does have its good points. It is almost completely insensitive to the form of the cost functions. We could have as many trades as desired, and additional constraints on the set of possible schedules help rather than complicate matters. However, the greatest advantage of dynamic programming's apparently brute-force approach to computation lies in all the extra work that we had to do in calculating the entire optimal value function table. Suppose for some reason the completion rates we ordered at some time are not achieved. We ordered r_1, r_2, r_3, but two weeks later we find we have achieved r_1', r_2' and r_3'. There is no need for recalculation. We simply refer to that part of the optimal value function table at stage n+1 corresponding to $(C_1+r_1', C_2+r_2', C_3+r_3')$ rather than the entry at $(C_1+r_1, C_2+r_2, C_3+r_3)$ where we expected to be. In short, we have the optimal set of schedules for whatever situation we get ourselves into. But this is exactly the information we need in order to fold back decision trees under uncertainty. And, of course, dynamic programming ability to handle decisions under uncertainty is the real reason why we have introduced the concept in the first place. In order to see how we can apply dynamic programming to decisions under uncertainty, we will return to our simple little network problem in the next section.

However, before we do this, we must comment on a basic error which has crept into the analysis of this problem. Given the above discussion of the computational feasiblity of this algorithm it is clear why the analyst viewed the more complete problem of the combined choice of *both* labor force levels and production schedules to be computationally infeasible. If the labor force variables were to be determined and not regarded as given, then in order to describe the state of the system we would need not only the present percent completions of each of the subs, but also the present levels of the labor force in each trade. If we had three trades and three subs, we would need six state variables and computationally the problem would be completely out of hand. So the analyst's decision to concentrate on the subproblem of determining the optimal production schedules *given* a specified level of each trade through time was a reasonable one. He could then vary the labor force parametrically and observe the results. However, given that the levels of each trade are fixed, regular time, 40-hour payroll costs are fixed and not subject to the choice of production schedule. From the point of view of the subproblem chosen for analysis, regular-time payroll costs are sunk; they cannot be varied. In fact, the only costs which are under control of the subproblem's decision variables are the overtime costs--these will vary with the choice of production schedules even if the regular-time labor force is fixed. By including the costs of undertime in his objective function, the analyst arrived at an algorithm which, blindly following his orders, often accepted a higher cost in overtime (a real loss to the yard) in order to save some undertime (a fictitious loss since the man gets paid the same whether he works or not). In short, once the problem was constrained to a choice of production schedules *given a specified labor force* only the cost of overtime should have been included in the objective function. The proper objective, given the problem statement, is that set of production schedules which minimizes overtime costs. The necessary adjustments to the recursion relations will be obvious to the reader. They involve merely leaving out the undertime terms.

The above error is a fairly subtle example of the quite common error of failure to distinguish which costs in a problem actually depend on the decisions being analyzed--in the economist's terms, failure to distinguish between fixed and variable costs, failure to realize that what are fixed costs for one decision are variable costs for another. As we have seen, such an error is not without real-world consequences. The reader by now has probably guessed that the misguided analyst in this particular problem was the author.

3.5 DYNAMIC PROGRAMMING UNDER UNCERTAINTY

In order to follow up on the earlier observation that somewhat brute-force approach of dynamic programming, which ends up
calculating the optimal strategy for every possible situation
we might get into, yields us just the information we need to
fold back decision trees under uncertainty, we return to the
simpler context of our little network problem. In Figure 3-5
we have reproduced Figure 3-1 with one exception. On each
branch emanating from every node we have placed a pair of additional numbers. The first such number represents the probability that we will actually traverse this branch if our decision
is to take it. The second number represents the probability
that we will take this path if our decision is to take its
alternate.

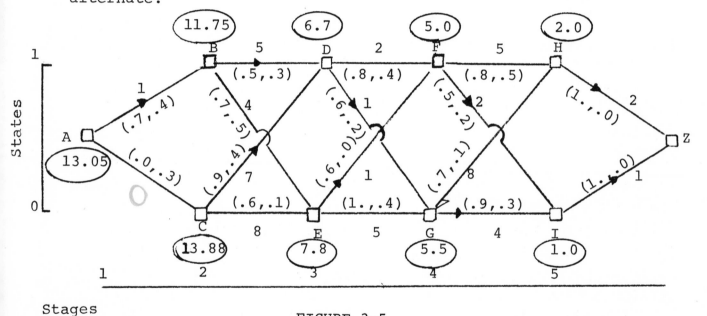

FIGURE 3-5

Thus, we might imagine the following process. After we get to
any node in the network, we somehow decide which branch we should
like to take. After making the decision, Nature (the weather,
labor unions, technical bugs, competitors) or some other perverse
object, flips a coin which says, "O.K., take the branch you
chose," with probability given by the first number in the pair

on that branch and with complementary probability says, "Sorry, go the other way." This complementary probability is the second number in the pair of the alternate branch. These probabilities may either be objective (based on large sample data) or subjective (based on the DM's betting odds).

Well, this is certainly a disheartening situation. We realize that we can no longer guarantee ourselves the minimum possible traversal cost of 9 as we could under certainty. In fact, we can say that, even if we pursue the formerly optimal strategy, we may suffer a relatively large cost while someone who does no thinking about the problem at all may be lucky and realize a lower cost. As we have seen, under uncertainty we must distinguish between a good decision and a good outcome. In order to identify good decisions we must specify an objective. A "good" decision then is one that is consistent with the specified objective.

For now let us assume that the DM's objective is to minimize the expected cost of traversing the network, that is, the DM is an EMV'er. We have already seen that this criterion implies a very specific attitude toward risk, an attitude to which most people do not subscribe. However, we have also seen that often the EMV'er's strategy is a reasonably good strategy for almost all DM's to follow especially if the amount risked is small with respect to the DM's asset position. Later we will apply DP to non-EMV preference functions. Unfortunately, this will involve a considerable increase in computational effort. Therefore, wherever possible we will attempt to fall back on expected value decision-making when using dynamic programming.

How can we use dynamic programming to calculate the strategy which leads to minimum expected cost? The key idea of dynamic programming is to think backwards. Start at the end of the problem and work forward. What is the optimal value of being at each of the last two nodes, H and I, given our new criterion? For these two nodes, the problem collapses. Neither we nor Nature has any choice and the expected cost of traversing

each of the last two links is 2 and 1 respectively. Thus,
the minimal expected cost for the rest of the process, given
that we are at node H (state 1 and stage 5), is 2 and the
minimal expected value of being in state 0 at stage 5 is 1.
Let us define a new optimal value function, denoted by $V_n(x_n)$
as before, but defined to be the minimum *expected* cost for
the remainder of the process if we are presently at stage n
and in state x_n. By this definition, $V_5(1)=2$; $V_5(0)=1$. We
are now ready to move back to stage 4 where things get a
little more interesting. Let us consider the situation given
that we are in state 1 at stage 4, i.e., we are at node F.
$V_4(1)$ is the minimum expected cost of getting from F to Z.
If at F we decide to take the upper branch, one of two things
can happen:

   (a) With likelihood .8 we go to H at a cost of 5;
   (b) With likelihood .2 we go to I at a cost of 2.

In either event we surely will do the best we can from
whatever state we end up in, but the value of the best we can
do in either of these two states is by definition $V_5(1)$ and
$V_5(0)$ respectively. Thus, the expected cost of taking the upper
branch at F and then doing the best we can, given whatever happens, is

$$.8\ [5+V_5(1)]+.2[2+V_5(0)]$$

which from above equals

$$.8(5+2)+.2(2+1)=6.2\ \ .$$

In a similar manner, we can obtain the expected cost of trying to take the lower branch from H. It is .5(2+1)+.5(5+2)=5.0.
But we wish to make that choice which minimizes the expected
cost of going from H to Z. Since 5.0<6.2 the indicated choice
is toward H and the minimum expected cost of this choice, the
optimal value associated with F, is 5.0. As before, we place
this value next to its node in a circle. Similarly, we can
calculate the minimum expected value associated with G, $V_4(0)$.

$$V_4(0) = \min \begin{cases} .7(8+2)+.3(4+1)=8.5 \\ \\ .9(4+1)+.1(8+2)=5.5 \end{cases}$$

$$= 5.5$$

and the indicated choice is the lower branch. By now the basic recursion should be clear. If we let $Pr(x_{n+1}|x_n,u)$ denote the probability of getting to state x_{n+1} at the next stage, given that we are presently in x_n and we choose the upper branch and if we let $Pr(x_{n+1}|x_n,d)$ equal the analogous quantity, given we choose the lower branch, the general recursion relation is

$$V_n(x_n) = \min \begin{cases} Pr(1|x_n,u)[c_u(x_n)+V_{n+1}(1)]+Pr(0|x_n,u)[c_d(x_n)+V_{n+1}(0)] \\ \\ Pr(0|x_n,d)[c_d(x_n)+V_{n+1}(0)]+Pr(1|x_n,d)[c_u(x_n)+V_{n+1}(1)] \end{cases}$$

Plugging $V_4(x_n)$ into this expression we calculate V_3 and so on.

Continuing on in this fashion, using the recursion, we work our way back to node A. The corresponding optimal value is 13.05. Despite the fact that the costs have not changed, we have lost on the average 4.05 units of cost per traversal due to the fact that we can no longer guarantee that our choices will be carried out. The optimal policy has also changed even though the underlying costs have not changed, demonstrating the obvious fact that our best choices under certainty are not necessarily our best choices under uncertainty even if we are EMV'ers. Note also that we cannot tell exactly what path we will take before the actual occurrence of the process. The exception is the first choice. We know we are going to choose to go up. However, after making this choice we have to wait to see what happens. After Nature makes her choice, then we can refer to the optimal value table and see which choice we should make, then it's Nature's turn, and so on. Under uncertainty, we can no longer write a program which not only computes the optimal value table working backwards, but also before the fact works forward through this table picking out the cost-minimizing choices. Under uncertainty, it doesn't make any sense to make up your mind before you have to. Dynamic programming accounts for this fact and generates a strategy through which we take advantage of the information which *will* be available to us at each stage in the future (in this case, what node we are at) and allows this information--the state of the system--to feed back on the decision which will be made at that time.

3.6 SUBMARINE PRODUCTION SCHEDULING UNDER UNCERTAINTY

We are now in a position to apply dynamic programming under uncertainty to the sub production scheduling problem. (We could also use it in the inventory problem where the prime uncertainty might be how many valves will actually be needed.) Let us restrict ourselves to the situation where between any two review periods only two things can happen. The ship progresses at some positive rate (say, 2% biweekly) or not at all. Also assume at each review period we have two alternatives--order production at the positive rate or order no production. In the latter case, we get no progress with probability 1.00. In the former case, we achieve our positive rate with probability $p_n(C_k)$, which may depend on the present state of completion, and we obtain no progress with probability $1-p_n(C_k)$.

Let $r_k=1$ mean that we order progress on sub k in the ensuing period and $r_k=0$ mean that we call for no construction on this sub during that time. Assuming that we choose to minimize expected value, the recursion for the optimal value function becomes:

$$V_n(C_1,C_2,C_3) = \min_{(r_1,r_2,r_3)} \begin{cases} \begin{aligned} & B_n(C_1,C_2,C_3;1,1,1) + \\ & p_n(C_1)p_n(C_2)p_n(C_3)V_{n+1}(C_1+r,C_2+r,C_2+r,C_3+r) \\ & +(1-p_n(C_1))p_n(C_2)p_n(C_3)V_{n+1}(C_1,C_2+r,C_3+r) \\ & +\ldots +\ldots +\ldots +\ldots +\ldots \\ & +(1-p_n(C_1))(1-p_n(C_2))(1-p_n(C_3))V_{n+1}(C_1,C_2,C_3) \end{aligned} \\ B_n(C_1,C_2,C_3;1,1,0) + \ldots \\ B_n(C_1,C_2,C_3;1,0,1) + \ldots \\ B_n(C_1,C_2,C_3;0,1,1) + \ldots \\ B_n(C_1,C_2,C_3;1,0,0) + \ldots \\ B_n(C_1,C_2,C_3;0,0,1) + \ldots \\ B_n(C_1,C_2,C_3;0,1,0) + \ldots \\ B_n(C_1,C_2,C_3;0,0,0) + V_{n+1}(C_1,C_2,C_3) \end{cases}$$

This is the basic recursion.* However, several modifications are in order with respect to boundary conditions. For one thing, we can no longer guarantee that we will with certainty meet the due date on each sub. Therefore, we must explicitly specify the penalties for not delivering on time and incorporate them into the stage return. That is, for all $C_k < 100\%$ and all $t_n > D_k$ then we must add an overdue penalty, $H(D_k - t_n)$ to the stage return. By making this penalty very large for large $D_k - t_n$ we can guarantee that a sub will be very late with low probability.

3.7 DYNAMIC PROGRAMMING FOR NON-EMV'ERS

Up to this point, in using the recursive reasoning of dynamic programming to help us fold back decision trees resulting from incomplete knowledge, we have assumed that the DM is an expected value decision-maker. Unfortunately, as we have seen, this is not always a tenable assumption. Many times a DM's risk preference constitutes the crux of the matter and must be included explicitly in the analysis.

---

*The B_n's in this expression have been modified by having the undertime terms deleted.

105

In this section, we shall see how we can use dynamic programming to help us fold back certain decision trees, given a non-EMVing preference function. To do so we will go back to our by-now-familiar little network problem. But now we will have to recast the problem slightly.

Let us suppose an investor has z units of wealth. These units might be in thousands or perhaps hundreds of thousands of dollars. Somehow he finds himself in the situation where he must traverse our little network from A to Z paying the associated costs in the same units of wealth. Our DM is a Bayesian, has accepted the axioms, and the probabilities shown in Figure 3-5 are his probabilities. We have obtained this DM's preference function for wealth over the range of 100 to 0 units. This function is shown in Figure 3-6. It exhibits considerable risk-adversion; however, this risk-adversion decreases with increase in wealth--that is, the premium that this DM would pay to insure himself against an unfavorable gamble decreases as his wealth increases. Our problem is to develop an algorithm which generates that strategy which gets our DM from A to Z in such a manner as to maximize the expected π-value associated with the DM's wealth after the traversal.*

Since the DM's risk adversion changes with his asset position, it is clear that we can no longer divide the overall costs of traversing the network into the immediate costs of traversing the next link and the costs which will be incurred in traversing the links further in the future and sum the two, just as in analyzing Joe's problem, given Joe's preference function, we were no longer able to assign a cost to a branch and add that cost to the cost of following a certain policy when we came to that branch in the folding-back process. Instead, we were forced to evaluate all the costs associated with a particular path through the tree, assign the total of these costs to the terminal node

---

*See reference 18 for a more detailed discussion of decreasing risk adversion.

FIGURE 3-6

A DECREASINGLY RISK ADVERSE PREFERENCE FUNCTION

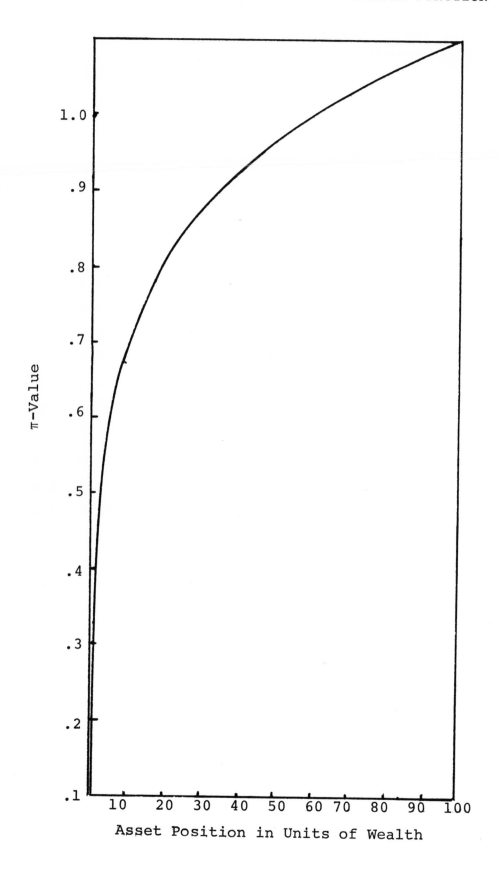

107

of the path, apply our preference function to this total, and then and only then start folding back. What we need is a device through which we can do the same thing and which at the same time allows us the computational advantages of dynamic programming.

Remember the definition of the state in the dynamic program: the information we need to know in order to make the next decision given the present stage. In the simple expected value network problem all we needed to know is where we are at the present stage. Given that knowledge, we were able to devise an expression for the costs of getting the rest of the way. Given a non-EMV'er's preference function, at each stage we need to know not only where we are, but also the DM's present wealth, given the costs he has already suffered, for changes in wealth will in general change his evaluation of the alternatives still facing him. Let the DM's present wealth at any stage be denoted by z. In order to see that knowledge of both the DM's whereabouts and his current wealth at any stage is sufficient to construct a recursion relation for the optimal value function we reason as follows.

Let us suppose the DM is presently at node H, that is, stage number 5 and at the upper node (x=1). Suppose further that the DM's present wealth after paying for the earlier portion of the trip is 10 units. Given this situation, the expected π-value-maximizing decision (the only decision in this case) is to take the remaining branch to z decreasing his wealth by 2 for a final wealth position of 8, which final outcome has a π-value of .57 (from Figure 3-6). Hence, the maximum expected π-value associated with node H, given z=10, is .57. We can repeat this simple computation for all possible z between 0 and 100 at H. Call the resulting list of numbers $V_5(1,z)$. We can do the same thing at I. Call this list $V_5(0,z)$. The lower portion of these two lists is shown in the following table.

TABLE 3-1

π-VALUES AT STAGE 5

z	$V_5(0,z)$	$V_5(1,z)$
2	.272	.000
3	.358	.272
4	.412	.358
5	.452	.412
6	.481	.452
7	.511	.484
8	.534	.511
9	.554	.534
10	.572	.554
.	.	.
.	.	.
.	.	.

We can now turn our attention to stage 4. Suppose the DM is at F and his present wealth is 12 units. What is his optimal choice, and what is it worth? He has two choices and, being a confirmed Bayesian, we know he wishes to make that choice which maximizes expected π-value. If he decides to go from F to H with probability .8 he will indeed go from F to H, in which case we will find that at stage 5, x=1 and z=12-5, but we know the maximum expected π-value associated with this state of affairs. From the rightmost column of Table 3-1, it is $V_5(1,7)=.484$. On the other hand, even if DM chooses to go from F to H, with probability .2 he will actually go to I and find himself in state (x=0,z=12-2) at n=5 which has an expected π-value of $V_5(0,10)=.572$ associated with it. Thus, the expected π-value associated with the choice to go from F to H given that the DM's wealth at F is 12 is:

$$.8(.484)+.2(.572)=.502 \quad .$$

Similarly, the expected π-value associated with the decision to go to I in this situation is:

$$.5(.572)+.5(.484)=.528$$

The optimal decision in this case is to attempt to go to I and the expected preference associated with this decision is

.528. This is the π-value of being at node F with 12 units of wealth. By a similar process, we can obtain the maximum expected π-value for each possible value of z at F and then for each possible value of z at G. It should be clear by now that we can repeat this process for D and E and then B and C and finally calculate the maximum expected preference associated with being at A for all possible z, i.e., all possible initial wealth positions.

This process can be described by the following set of recursion relations. Define $V_n(x,z)$ to be the maximum expected preference attainable if at stage n we are at node x and our present wealth is z units. then the boundary condition is $V_5(x,z)=\pi(z)$ for x=0,1 and all possible z while for stages 5 through 1 we have

$$V_n(x,z)=\max \begin{cases} Pr(1|x_n,u)V_{n+1}(1,z+c_d(x_n))+Pr(0|x_n,u)\cdot V_{n+1}(0,z+c_d(x_n)) \\ \\ Pr(0|x_n,d)V_{n+1}(0,z+c_d(x_n))+Pr(1|x_n,d)V_{n+1}(1,z+c_u(x_n)) \end{cases}$$

The top line of the right-hand side of this expression is the best we can do in terms of expected π-value if we decide to go up at n and x; the bottom line is best we can do if we choose to go down.

Notice that this recursion relation has no immediate costs, the effect of the immediate cost being accommodated by the change in the (expanded) set of state variables from which state variables we can calculate the preference associated with the path when we come to the terminal node as the boundary condition indicates. In control theory terms we have transformed the problem into a terminal control problem--a problem in which the value of the objective is a function only of the terminal state. Almost any sequential optimization problem can be transformed into a terminal control problem by suitable expansion of the state space. However, in general, whenever the objective function is separable, as it is for the EMV'er, this is unnecessary and computationally unwise, for as is clear from this example expanding the state space generally increases computational effort and demands on memory spaces combinatorially. In the simple problem at hand, it has increased computational effort over 100-fold.

However, the extra effort is not completely without compensation for when we are finished we will have calculated the maximum expected π-value and by implication the corresponding policy for all possible initial wealth positions. The DM can determine his optimal strategy by entering the optimal value function table at stage 1 with his initial wealth, whatever it may be, choosing to take that decision for which equality holds in the above equation, then wait and see what Nature does at stage 1, and then refer to the entries in the optimal value function table corresponding to the state that results. And so on.

The optimal value function table associated with the preference function of Figure 3-6 has been calculated. In this case, it turns out that no matter what the DM's initial wealth position is between 25 and 100 he should follow the EMV'er's policy, as shown by the arrows in Figure 3-5. For this network, the EMV'er's policy not only maximizes expected monetary value, but happens also to be a low-risk policy. This will not be true in general. If a DM were sufficiently risk-prone he would switch back to the optimum policy under certainty which gives him a slightly higher change at the minimum of all possible losses 9 than the EMV'er's strategy does.

If the results of these policy calculations are hardly earthshaking, the optimal value table itself still holds some interest. Consider Table 3-2, which shows a range of maximum expected preference values at node A over a range of initial wealths together with the corresponding certainty monetary equivalent.

The final column in this table shows the difference between his initial wealth and the CME associated with his optimal strategy. This is the amount this DM is willing to pay to avoid having to traverse the network. Note that for high initial wealths the DM is for all practical purposes an EMV'er for the

111

TABLE 3-2

z	$V_1(\cdot, z)$	CME	z-CME
25	.617	10.9	14.1
50	.811	36.7	13.3
75	.907	61.9	13.1
100	.973	87.05	13.05

expected cost of traversing the network is about 13.05 units. However, for low initial wealths, the DM is willing to pay a premium of the order of ten percent of the expected cost of traversing to avoid the risks entailed. There is always the possibility he will be very unlucky and suffer the maximum possible cost which is 23 units, which if his initial wealth is only 25 would just about wipe him out. Behavior such as that shown in Table 3-2 is what we mean by decreasing risk adversion. Of course, many people do not exhibit decreasing risk adversion.

This completes our introduction to dynamic programming. In the following chapters, we will attempt to use this often powerful technique to address some of the complex sequences of decisions facing marine decision-makers.

CHAPTER 4

INVESTMENT IN MARINE TRANSPORTATION

In this chapter we will attempt to apply the methodology
of Chapters 2 and 3 to investment in marine shipping services, to the buying and leasing of ships. Unlike the problem
we made up for our hypothetical friend Joe, in marine transportation the most important uncertainties are not on the cost
side but rather on the revenue side. Such uncertainties take
their purest form in the ship charter markets. The ship charter
markets are the arenas where buyers (oil companies, grain and
ore exporters, large-scale shippers in general) and sellers
(shipowners) bid for and offer ship services for varying lengths
of time. The contracts or leases consummated in these markets
are called *charters* or *fixtures*. The vessel which is leased is
said to be *chartered*.

These markets are in many respects the most interesting and
certainly the most volatile economic phenomena associated with
marine decision-making, combining the romanticism of the sea
with a cast of actors which include some of the world's wealthi-
est and most publicized men. Few commodity prices fluctuate as
violently as the unit prices in these markets which are called
the *charter rates*. The *spot tanker rate*, the unit price of an
immediate, single-voyage rental of a tanker, has been known to
increase (decrease) by as much as 500% in a matter of months.
As a result, immense fortunes can be made and lost in these markets in very short order. These fluctuations depend in an unpre-
dictable manner on the policies of unstable governments, the
location of future discoveries of oil and minerals or, in the
grain markets, the vagaries of the monsoon, and the ship-order-
ing policies of fellow shipowners. Clearly, in the ship charter
markets we have an ideal subject for our ideas on how to handle
uncertainty.

4.1 THE INDEPENDENT OWNER'S OPERATING ALTERNATIVES

We will begin by studying the vessel employment alternatives facing an independent shipowner operating in, say, the

tanker charter market.* After all, we cannot logically decide
whether or not to invest in a ship until we have some idea how
we would operate this ship if it were bought and what we would
obtain from these operations. Perhaps the first analytical
treatment of the ship employment problem was by Svendsen, reference 19. Svendsen assumed a somewhat simpler cost structure
than we will use and, more importantly, he assumed no uncertainty. He concluded, however, by pointing out that quantities
which cannot be predicted with certainty were of overriding
importance. "...it will be seen that these known factors do
not play such an important role in the calculations as do the
estimates on what the future holds." More recently, Mossin,
reference 14, tackled the layup problem under the assumption
that revenues (charter rates) were given by a symmetric random
walk. Given a simple cost structure, this hypothesis and EMVing
leads to decision rules of the form: lay up when rates drop
below x, come out of layup when rates rise above y. For the
more general situations considered herein, such rules will not
in general be optimal.

We begin by considering, with Svendsen, a single vessel
operating in a charter market which may be used in only one
trade and on only one route. We might, for example, imagine a
tanker which for some reason is restricted to the Persian Gulf-
Northern European run. Since 60% of tanker ton-miles move on
this route and, more importantly, since the rates on other routes
will tend to equilibrate at levels which return the owner of a
particular tanker the same amount on every route,** this may

---

* An independent owner is one who has no proprietary shipping
  requirements of his own.

**Of course, one has to base the computations on the right route
  for the ship in question. For example, in the winter months,
  a shallow draft tanker ('<38') can generally earn considerably
  more on the Venezuela-Delaware Bay route--a route this class
  of tankers has to itself--than it can be competing with the
  big guys on a deep draft route. In general, one should choose
  as the route upon which to base the calculations a route upon
  which the ship is as profitable as on any other route.

not be as confining an assumption as it might at first appear. This restriction will allow us to assume that the duration of a round-trip voyage is a constant, say, ΔN months. We further assume that every ΔN months, that is, at the completion of every round-trip voyage period, the ship's owner reviews the present situation with respect to the charter market and the status of his ship and decides which of the alternatives available to him at that review period he is actually going to follow. Let us begin by assuming that the ship's owner is an EMV'er and, therefore, his objective is to operate the ship through time in such a manner as to yield maximum expected present valued profit.* Later on we will tackle the non-EMV'er's problem.

In general, the alternatives open to the shipowner at the end of any round-trip period will depend on the present status of his ship. If at any review period the ship is laid up, his alternatives are: leave the ship in layup, bring it out of lay-up, and charter the ship for 1,2, or more voyage periods or scrap the ship.** If the ship is presently in commission and is not already fixed at the time of the review, he can charter it for any of a number of voyage periods: hold the ship on berth (not accept present charter rates), lay it up, or scrap it. If the ship is operating but is already committed at the current review period, then he has no immediate alternatives. In real life, he can accept any of the number of forward chartering contracts which may be offered him, committing his ship still further into the future.*** If, at what would be a review

---

* Present value is defined on page 121 Readers not familiar with the concept should consult any *recent* book on capital investment.

** More generally, the final option is the sell the ship. Here we are assuming that, if the ship is expected to at least recover variable costs in the future, the market sales value capitalizes these earnings, so only if the ship expects to be unprofitable will the DM wish to sell, in which case sales price equals scrap value.

***A forward charter is a fixture commencing some time in the future.

point, the ship has already been scrapped, then the owner has, of course, no options with respect to the particular ship in question.

Thus, in actual fact there is in general a rich variety of options open to the shipowner at any particular review point. However, in our abstraction of this problem we are going to have to limit somewhat these options. Specifically, we will rule out forward chartering. This simplification can be replaced by other more general sets of assumptions, if desired, but the exposition of the resulting algorithm becomes quite cumbersome. Under the above restriction, the set of charter alternatives can be represented by M different options corresponding to accepting an m-voyage charter where m runs from 1, the spot charter, to some maximum charter length in voyage periods M*. Given this restricted set of options, the status of the owner's ship at any review point, t_n, can be represented by a variable X running from -2 to M-1 defined by

$X = -2$ if ship has already been scrapped at t_n

$X = -1$ if ship is presently laid up at t_n

$X = \ 0$ if ship is available for immediate charter at t_n

$X = \ k$ $1 \leq k \leq M-1$ if ship has k voyages left on present contract

Given this notation and the above restrictions, the options available at any review point as a function of X are:

Status of Ship	Alternatives
X = -2	None
X = -1	Leave laid up, recommission
X = 0	Lay up, hold on berth, charter for k voyage periods, scrap
X = k $1 \leq k \leq M-1$	None

---

*We can pick any M we like. However, as we shall see, computational effort grows with the square of $M/\Delta N$. In a typical problem, ΔN might be 2 and M=30 or five years. That is, if M=30 and ΔN=2, we have allowed the owner the options of chartering for pretty much any length of time between two months and five years.

116

4.2 THE STATE OF THE MARKET

In making the decision at any review point, the shipowner will note not only the present status of his ship, but also the present state of the relevant charter market as well as his present feelings about the future. Now there are a number of approaches one might take to describing the present state of the market and incorporating the shipowner's hard-won experience and knowledge concerning the market into the problem. In this chapter we shall discuss two possible approaches:

1) A formulation of the problem based directly on the current value of the spot charter rate.

2) A formulation based on the demand and supply variables upon which the rates depend.

4.3 A MARKOVIAN MODEL OF THE CHARTER RATES

The approach through a model based directly on the spot rate is conceptually the simpler of the two, so let's start with it. In using this tack, we ask the DM to choose a (very small) number of variables which, *as far as he is concerned*, describe the present state of the market at any particular review time and upon which he is willing to base his feelings about where the market will be at the next review point. He might, for example, choose the following three variables.

1) The current spot charter rate at t_n, $R_1(n)$;*

2) The rate of change of the spot rate $\Delta R_1 = R_1(n) - R_1(n-1)$;

3) The amount of transport capability on order as measured by the time to launch in voyage periods, L, of a ship ordered in the present review period.

Other combinations of market variables can be used but this is as good as any place to start.

In order to make the size of the state space finite, we will have to assume that R_1 is a discrete variable. That is,

---

*When speaking about the current values of state variables we will suppress the stage argument unless it is not completely redundant, that is, generally we will write R_1 for the current value of the spot rate rather than $R_1(n)$.

117

assume that the shipowner is willing to act as if only a finite number of spot rates are possible, for example, $5.00/ton, $6.00/ton,...$15.00/ton. In other words the owner is willing to round off the spot rate to the nearest dollar or, if need be, to the nearest 50 cents. If this is the case, then ΔR_1 being the difference of two discrete variables is also discrete.

Now, in order to make a decision between a single-voyage charter and an m-voyage charter, we will need to know the current m-voyage charter rate, R_m.* This problem could be handled by adding R_m for all possible m to our list of state variables. However, this has obvious computational disadvantages which we would prefer to avoid. Zannetos, reference 22, has made an extensive empirical investigation of the behavior of term charter rates. He postulates that the important variables determining their value at any time are:

1) The current spot rate, R_1
2) The rate of change of the spot rate, ΔR_1**
3) The backlog, L
4) The duration of the charter, m
5) The size of the vessel,_____
6) The amount of the fleet presently idle
7) Change in amount of the fleet idle
8) New orders
9) Lead time between charter agreement and vessel delivery

Variable 9 he finds to have no significant effect on the term rates. Besides, it presumes forward chartering which we have ruled out. In the next section, we will argue that variables 7 and 8 are dependent on variables 1 and 2, in the sense that, if one knows the spot rates at t_n and t_{n-1}, then one can

---

* We are tacitly assuming that the term charter is of the consecutive voyage variety. This involves no loss in generality since, once a route has been specified, regular term charter rates can be transformed into equivalent consecutive voyage rates and vice versa.

**Actually Zannetos used a discounted sum of the rate changes observed in the last four periods with a discount factor which was large enough so that the resulting index, like ΔR_1, is mainly a function of the difference between $R_1(n)$ and $R_1(n-1)$.

estimate the amount of the fleet that is idle at these two points in time quite closely. Finally, Zoller, reference 23, has found that variable 6, the amount of tonnage ordered in a particular period, is primarily a function of the current spot rate and the size of the order book. In short, ruling out variable 9, we are suggesting that of the first eight variables only the first five can usefully be regarded as independent and hence a model of the long-term rates based on the first eight variables is essentially a model based on the first five. But the current values of the first five variables are known at any combination of stage and state and alternative charter length. Hence, from these five variables, we can use the Zannetos model to predict the present values of the term charter rates. In sum, we assume that the DM is willing to postulate two functions:

1) $O(R_1, \Delta R_1, L)$ which yields the DM's estimate of the amount of tonnage which will be ordered by the ship-owners operating in his charter market in the present voyage period.

2) $R_m(R_1, \Delta R_1, L)$ which yields the DM's estimate of the m-voyage charter rate which will exist in the market for his ship if the current spot rate, rate of change of the spot rate, and launch time is $(R_1, \Delta R_1, L)$.

4.4 THE ALGORITHM

With all the above assumptions, we are in a position to develop a dynamic program for determining that vessel employment policy which will return maximum expected present valued profits to the owner. Given the above description of the market, at any decision point, t_n, the present state of the ship/market system is described by the value of the vector $(X, R_1, \Delta R_1, L)$. Let n be the age of the ship in voyage periods. Let N by the maximum age of the ship in voyage periods which we will consider. That is, N is an age so old that the probability that the ship will reach that age before we have scrapped it is insignificant. To put a boundary condition on the problem, we will arbitrarily assume that if the ship reaches age N we will scrap it no matter

119

what the present state of the market is. If an N corresponding to, say, 30 years is chosen, such a restriction will have very little effect on the resulting policy.

Associated with each of the alternatives at any particular combination of stage and state are differing revenues and outlays. These are tabulated below:

$B(n)$ — Net scrap value of the ship at age n in voyage periods.

$C_L(n)$ — Cost of laying up the ship at age n.

$C_R(n)$ — Cost of recommissioning an n-voyage period old ship. For simplicity of exposition, we will assume that it takes ΔN to put the ship in or take it out of layup. (Other assumptions can be handled without introducing any great computational problems.)

$C_M(n)$ — Cost of maintaining a laid-up ship for a period ΔN.

$C_H(n)$ — Cost of holding a ship on berth for a period ΔN.

$C_V(n,m)$ — Present value of *voyage* costs associated with an m-voyage charter.

All these costs should be actual cash flow expenses associated with the maintenance and operation of the ship. They should not include any costs which do not depend on the employment decisions. In particular, they should not include any capital charges. Notice that all the above costs may depend on the age of the ship so that rising maintenance or fuel costs or periodic survey costs can be included on the model as well as changes in price levels through time (inflation) as desired.

Let t_n be the point in time corresponding to a ship age of n round-trip voyage periods. At any such decision point, the state of things has been characterized by the present status of the ship, X, and the present state of the market $(R_1, \Delta R_1, L)$. For every possible combination of age n, and state of the system $(X, R_1, \Delta R_1, L)$, we define the following optimal value function:

$W_n(X, R_1, \Delta R_1, L)$ = maximum expected present valued profit achievable from the ship for the remainder of its life given that the ship is presently n round-trip voyage periods old and the state of the system is $(X, R_1, \Delta R_1, L)$.*

Our job is to develop a recursion relationship for W_n. This relationship takes on a differing form depending on the value of X.

If the ship has already been scrapped at t_n, (X=-2), then there is no profit achievable from this ship in the future. Hence,

$$W_n(-2, R_1, \Delta R_1, L) = 0 \qquad\qquad (4.1)$$

If the ship is presently laid up at t_n, (X=-1), then we have three options: scrap it, leave it in layup, and recommission. If we scrap the ship, we will receive B(n) and the decision sequence will end. If we leave the ship in layup, then in the interval (t_n, t_{n+1}), we will experience an outlay of $C_M(n)$ and at the next decision point, t_{n+1}, we will find ourselves in state $(-1, R_1(n+1), \Delta R_1(n+1), L(n+1))$ where $R_1(n+1)$, and $\Delta R_1(n+1)$, the value of the spot rate one period hence and its rate of change are not known with certainty at t_n. In order to take expectations over these random variables, we require that our Bayesian owner has, from his long experience with the market, developed subjective probabilities on the likelihood of the various possible values of the spot charter rate at t_{n+1} given the state

---

*Let R_i and C_i be the cash inflow and cash outflow in period i. The present value at period n, PV(n), of a time stream of such flows between period n and period m further in the future is

$$PV(n) = \sum_{k=0}^{m-n} \rho^k (R_{n+k} - C_{n+k})$$

where $\rho = (1+i)^{-1}$, i being the DM's opportunity cost of capital-- the loss associated with tying up a unit of capital for a period. From this definition, we have the following recursion which we will make frequent use of.

$$PV(n) = (R_n - C_n) + \sum_{k=1}^{m-n} \rho^k (R_{n+k} - C_{n+k})$$

$$= (R_n - C_n) + \rho PV(n+1)$$

The argument for using present value to account for the time value of money can be found in any text on capital budgeting.

of the market at t_n. Precisely, we required the owner's $\Pr(R(n+1)|R(n),\Delta R(n),L(n))$ for all possible values of the four arguments. In Chapter 6 we shall outline how a Bayesian would use past market history to obtain these probabilities. Given these probabilities, the expectation of the maximum present valued profit obtainable from the ship *from* t_{n+1} *on*, given that we leave the ship in layup at t_n is

$$\sum_{R_1(n+1)} \Pr(R_1(n+1)|R_1(n),\Delta R_1(n),L(n)) W_{n+1}(-1,R_1(n+1,R_1(n+1)-R_1(n),L(n+1))$$

where $L(n+1)=L(n)+\Delta L(0(R_1(n),\Delta R_1(n),L(n)))$ where ΔL is the change in time to launch associated with new orders amounting to $0(R_1,\Delta R_1 L)$. A more concise way of writing the above summation is

$$E[W_{n+1}(-1,R_1(n+1),\Delta R_1(n+1),L(n+1))|R_1(n),\Delta R_1(n),L(n)]$$

Summing up, the maximum expected present valued profit *from* t_n *on*, given the state of the system at t_n is $(-1,R_1,\Delta R_1,L)$ and the ship is left in layup is

$$-C_M(n)+\rho E[W_{n+1}(-1,R_1(n+1),\Delta R_1(n+1),L(n+1))|R_1(n),\Delta R_1(n),L(n)]$$

where ρ is the discount factor relevant to the interval ΔN and shipowner's opportunity cost of capital. If, on the other hand, the owner decides to recommission his ship at t_n given $(-1,R_1 \Delta R_1,L)$, then in the interval (t_n, t_{n+1}) the owner will experience the costs of bringing the ship out of layup, $C_R(n)$, and at t_{n+1} he will find himself in state $(0,R_1(n+1), \Delta R_1(n+1),L(n+1))$, i.e., the ship will be in commission and available for charter. Thus, the maximum expected present valued profit associated with the option of recommissioning the ship at t_n, given that the present state is $(-1,R_1,\Delta R_1,L)$ is

$$-C_R(n)+\rho E[W_{n+1}(0,R_1(n+1),\Delta R_1(n+1),L(n+1))|R_1(n),\Delta R_1(n),L(n)]$$

Putting this all together with the realization that if the ship is laid up at t_n, the EMVing owner will choose that alternative which maximizes future expected present valued profits and, if he does so, the resulting expected profit from t_n on will be $W_n(-1,R_1 \; R_1,L)$ we have

$$W_n(-1,R_1,\Delta R_1,L)=\max\begin{cases} B(n) \\ -C_M(n)+\rho E[W_{n+1}(-1,R_1(n+1),\Delta R_1(n+1)L(n+1))\,|\,R_1\Delta R_1,L] \\ -C_R(n)+\rho E[W_{n+1}(0,R(n+1),\Delta R_1(n+1)L(n+1))\,|\,R_1,\Delta R_1 L] \end{cases}$$

$$(4.2)$$

If the ship is currently operational and available for charter, that is, if X=0, then the owner has M+3 options: scrap, layup, hold on berth, or charter for m-voyage periods, $1\leq m\leq M$. If he scraps the ship he will receive B(n) and the decision sequence ends. If he lays the ship up, he will bear the cost of layup and, at the next stage, X will equal -1. Hence, the maximum expected present valued profit associated with layup is

$$-C_L(n)+\rho E[W_{n+1}(-1,R_1(n+1),\Delta R_1(n+1,L(n+1))\,|\,R_1,\Delta R_1,L]$$

If he refuses to accept any of the prevailing rates and holds the ship on berth, then he will bear the costs of holding the ship on berth for a period ΔN and, at t_{n+1}, X will equal 0. Hence, the value associated with this option is:

$$-C_H(n)+\rho E[W_{n+1}(0,R_1(n+1),\Delta R_1(n+1),L(n+1))\,|\,R_1,\Delta R_1,L]$$

If he accepts an m-voyage charter, then he assures himself of a revenue stream whose present value (discounted back to t_n) is

$$\hat{R}_m = \sum_{k=0}^{m-1} \rho^k R_m(R_1,\Delta R_1,L)$$

and at the same time commits himself to an operating cost stream whose present value is

$$\hat{C}_m = \sum_{k=0}^{m} \rho^k C_v(n)$$

Hence, if we, somewhat like an accountant, count costs and revenues at the time we become irrevocably committed to the corresponding outlays and incomes, then the maximum expected present valued profit associated with accepting an m-voyage charter at t_n, given that the current state is $(0, R_1, \Delta R_1, L)$ is

$$\hat{R}_m - \hat{C}_m + \rho E[W_{n+1}(m-1, R_1(n+1), \Delta R_1(n+1), L(n+1)) | R_1, \Delta R_1, L]$$

where the m-1 indicates that at stage n+1 we will have m-1 voyage still to go on the current charter contract.

Putting this all together we have the expression for the maximum expected present valued profit from t_n on given $(0, R_1, \Delta R_1 L)$:

$$W_n(0, R_1, \Delta R_1, L) = \max \begin{cases} B(n) \\ -C_L(n) + \rho E[W_{n+1}(-1, R_1(n+1), \Delta R_1(n+1), L(n+1)) | R_1, \Delta R_1, L] \\ -C_H(n) + \rho E[W_{n+1}(0, R_1(n+1) \Delta R_1(n+1), L(n+1)) | R_1, \Delta R_1, L] \\ \hat{R}_m - \hat{C}_m + E[W_{n+1}(m-1, R_1(n+1), \Delta R_1(n+1), L(n+1)) | R_1, \Delta R_1, L] \end{cases}$$

$$m = 1, 2, \ldots, M \qquad (4.3)$$

Notice that in this situation the owner will accept a spot charter (m=1) rather than hold on berth if and only if $R_1 - C_v < C_H$ since both of these alternatives result in the same expected profits from t_{n+1} on. That is, for these two alternatives considered in isolation conventional marginal cost reasoning still holds. This is, in part, because our problem formulation does not give the "hold at berth" alternative full credit for its flexibility, since we have allowed the DM to review the situation *only* at the points $(\ldots, t_n, t_{n+1}, \ldots)$. The shorter we make the review period the less serious this restriction becomes.

Finally we have to consider the case of $X \geq 1$ at t_n. If X is greater than zero, since we have ruled out forward chartering, the owner has no immediate options at t_n. The owner can only sit back, collect his term charter payment (for which we have already given him credit) and pay his voyage expenses (which also have already been accounted for). Hence, for $1 \leq X \leq M-1$, we have

$$W_n(X, R_1, \Delta R_1, L) = \rho E[W_{n+1}(X-1, R_1(n+1), \Delta R_1(n+1), L(n+1)) | R_1, \Delta R_1, L]$$

$$(4.4)$$

It should now be clear why we credited the owner for the entire present value of his term charter net revenue stream when he made the decision to accept the charter for when we compute W_n backwards we will have no way of knowing what the term charter rate was when the ship was originally chartered.

The above set of recursion relations, Equations 4.1, 4.2, 4.3 and 4.4 hold for all n between 0 and N-1 inclusive. At ship age N, by assumption, the only option is to scrap the ship if it has not already been scrapped. Hence,

$$W_N(-2, R_1, \Delta R_1, L) = 0$$

$$W_N(X, R_1, \Delta R_1, L) = B(N) \quad \text{for} \quad -1 \leq X \leq M-1 \tag{4.5}$$

Equation 4.5 is the boundary condition. The computation proceeds in a straightforward dynamic programming manner, substituting the boundary condition into the r.h.s. of 4.1 through 4.4 and substituting the resulting left-hand side recursively into the right-hand side. If we describe the market by ten spot charter rates, ten possible rates of change, 20 different launch times, and N=2 months (Persian Gulf-Northern Europe) and M=18 (3 years) the size of the state space is about 40,000-- large but not out of the question, given the large amounts at stake.

4.5 SHIP INVESTMENT

An important application of this algorithm might be in determining the desirability of investing in a ship for use in the charter market. This would be done in the following manner.

Let us suppose, if we order a ship now, it will be launched L_o round-trip voyage periods from now. Let this launch time be n=0. (That is, now, the time of our decision whether or not to order a ship is $t=-L_o \cdot \Delta N$. Calculate $W_0(\cdot, R_1(0), \Delta R_1(0), L(0))$ for all possible combinations of $(R_1(0), \Delta R_1, L)$ by Equation 4.4. The dot in place of the ship status variable indicates that this variable is not relevant to the construction period.

$W_{-L_O}(\cdot, R_1(-L_O)), \Delta R_1(-L_O), L(-L_O), L(-L_O)$ is the expected operating profit obtained from the ship if launched at n=0 present valued back to $n=-L_O$ (now) given that the state of the market at $n=-L_O$ is $(R_1(-L_O), \Delta R_1(-L_O), L(-L_O))$. Next calculate the present value of the stream of fixed outlays associated with the decision to purchase the ship $\hat{C}_F$. This cost stream will include the capital cost of the ship, adjusted by financing arrangements, fixed operating and salary costs--any ship-related costs left out of the operating costs defined earlier. Taxes should be treated just like any other outlays. (No share of company overhead costs which would be incurred whether or not the ship is built should be included. All those overhead costs which will be incurred if the ship is built but not incurred if not should be included.) If $\hat{C}_F < W_{-L_O}(\cdot, R_1(-L_O), \Delta R_1(-L_O), L(-L_O))$ then the EMV'er should order the ship. Otherwise he should not. Notice, without recalculating the basic optimal value function table, we have the optimal ship ordering policy for a large number of combinations of stages and states. In short, in solving the optimal employment problem one solves the optimal vessel purchase policy problem. We have, of course, assumed that market rate behavior is independent of the shipowner's ordering decisiion. For a large owner, this might not be true.

Notice also that for an EMV'er the fixed cost associated with purchasing and owning the ship does not affect the optimal operating policy. Once the ship is built these costs are invariant or, in the vernacular, sunk. The cost of construction certainly influences whether or not a ship should be built. However, *once the ship is built*, the owner must do the best he can from where he is and not allow artificial accounting concepts such as depreciation or "fully allocated" costs to influence his operating decisions.

4.6 A DEMAND EXOGENOUS-SUPPLY ENDOGENOUS MODEL

The preceding approach to the vessel employment problem was based directly on the prevailing spot rate. Now the charter rates, and the spot rate in particular, are not the driving

126

forces in these markets. Rather they are determined by the underlying demand for and supply of the type of shipping services which the owner has to offer.

Any experienced owner has quite a bit of knowledge concerning these underlying supply and demand variables. The preceding model does not allow the owner to incorporate this knowledge into his calculations except indirectly. Therefore, let us see if we cannot develop a ship employment algorithm based directly on the demand and supply variables relevant to a vessel charter market. As we shall see, such an algorithm has both advantages and disadvantages with respect to the rate-based model. This exercise will also serve to demonstrate that, when one is confronted with a real-world problem, there is generally a large number of ways of tackling it. The art of analysis involves choosing that computationally-feasible approach which is most appropriate to the problem *and the DM* at hand. Consider the following three market state variables:

1) A variable specifying the present short-run demand function for the kind of shipping services (tanker, dry bulk, general cargo) which the owner's ship provides, D.

2) A variable relating to the present short-run supply function of this type of ships, S.

3) A variable specifying the amount of this type of ship which is presently on order or under construction in the yards of the world, L.

These are the three most important structural variables underlying both the behavior of the market rates and the industry's decision to expand supply. We will take each in turn.

In most vessel charter markets and particularly in the important tanker market, the short-run demand for shipping services is quite inelastic, that is, the ton-miles of ship services demanded in a certain period, say, ΔN, is largely insensitive to the current charter rates. Large-scale shippers, such as

oil companies and ore processors, are rather tightly committed
to obtaining a smooth flow of shipments, which flow it pays them
to maintain even if the charter rates change rather drastically.
This fixity in turn is derived from the short-run inelasticity
of the final markets for such basic products as oil, steel,
aluminum, grain, etc. The situation is roughly that shown in
Figure 4.1 where the quantity of transportation demanded, q_d
through period ΔN, depends only very weakly on the current value
of the charter rate, r. In such a case we can usefully speak
of a *level* of demand, D. D is the ton-miles demanded by shippers in the current review period. Notice that, while the D
that exists in any given period is for all practical purposes
independent of the current rate, this does not mean that before
the fact we know what D is. Quite the contrary, the level of
demand in ton-miles which will exist in future periods is the
single biggest uncertainty in this problem.*

While the amount of transport service demanded is quite
insensitive to the existing rate, the amount of such service
which the industry will be willing to supply $q_s(r)$ will, over
certain ranges of r, be critically sensitive to the rate. In
shipping markets, the behavior of transportation supply offered
will look like that shown in Figure 4.2. If the market rate
is below some minimum value, r, no shipowner will find it to
his advantage to accept the rate for the *additional* costs associated with the voyage will be greater than the revenues he
earns from the voyage. As the rates rise, a point will be
reached where the most efficient vessels will make more money
if they accept the rate than if they do not. If the rates continue to rise, more and more vessels will find it to their advantage to accept charters and rather quickly most of the fleet
will become employed. This is represented by the steeply-rising

---

*Notice that we are speaking of demand for shipping, demand
in ton-miles. The demand for oil in tons can be reasonably
well predicted over at least the medium term. However, the
demand for tankship services depends on where this oil comes
from and by what route, which depends on such scarcely predictable factors as location of new finds, U.S. quota policies,
the Arab-Israeli conflicts, etc.

portion of the curve in Figure 4.2. After most of the fleet is
employed, only very old or very inefficient ships or ships de-
signed for some other trade will be called into activity by further rises in the rates and the supply curve begins to level
off. After these latter ships are operating, the only way supply can be increased further is by operating above design
speeds, by working overtime shifts in ports, etc. These are
very expensive measures which have only a slight effect on
transportation supply. At this point the supply curve becomes
quite insensitive to further increases in the rate. Empirical
investigations by Zannetos, reference 22, indicate that the tanker supply curve can be approximated by

$$q_s = S \cdot (96.75 - 2.5.5/r^2)$$

where S is the total amount of design capacity of the fleet and
r is the spot rate in cents per 1,000 ton-miles. Devanney and
Lassiter, reference 3, have estimated the short-run supply function by computing additional voyage costs for the present (1970)
tanker fleet. Both these approximations are shown in Figure 4.2.
Clearly, whatever form of the supply curve is chosen, the
key variable is the total transport capacity currently afloat,
S. In short, we are suggesting that, if one knows the current
value of S, one has to a large degree ascertained the current
short-run supply function. But if one knows both the current
level of demand, D, and the current design capacity of the
fleet, S, that is, if one knows the current short-run demand
and supply functions, then one can predict the current spot
rate for the market rate will be that rate at which the supply
offered equals the transport services demanded, the rate R_1
at which

$$q_d(R_1, D) = q_s(R_1, S)$$

or solving for the spot rate

$$R_1 = H(D, S)$$

where the function H will depend on the form of the supply and

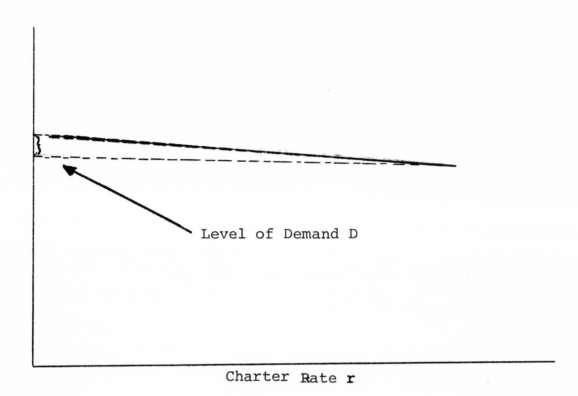

Ton-Miles Demanded in Present Quarter q_D

Level of Demand D

Charter Rate r

FIGURE 4.1

SHORT RUN DEMAND CURVE

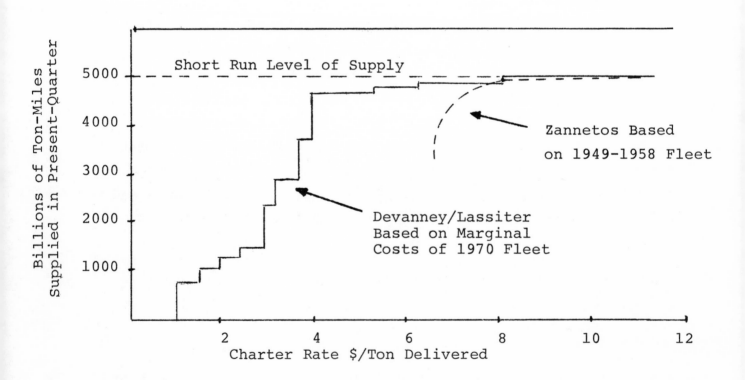

Billions of Ton-Miles Supplied in Present-Quarter

Short Run Level of Supply

Zannetos Based
on 1949-1958 Fleet

Devanney/Lassiter
Based on Marginal
Costs of 1970 Fleet

Charter Rate $/Ton Delivered

FIGURE 4.2

SHORT RUN LEVEL OF SUPPLY

demand functions assumed. Thus, if one knows D and S one can obtain at least an estimate of R_1.*

The variable L has already been discussed in relationship to the rate-based algorithm.

But if one has R_1 and L and *one is willing to disregard the effect of the rate of change of the spot rate*, then by earlier arguments one can develop estimates of the current term rates $\{R_m : m=2, \ldots M\}$ and of the transport capability ordered in the present voyage period $0(R_1, L)$. If this is the case, we are in a position to develop an algorithm based on the four state variables (X,D,S,L) which develops the vessel employment strategy consistent with these assumptions and maximum expected present valued profit.

In fact, by reasoning exactly similar to that used earlier

$$W(-2,D,S,L)=0$$

$$W(-1,D,S,L)=\max \begin{cases} B(n) \\ -C_m(n)+\rho E[W_{n+1}(-1,D(n+1),S(n+1),L(n+1))|D,S,L)] \\ -C_R(n)+\rho E[W_{n+1}(0,D(n+1),S(n+1),L(n+1))|D(n),S(n),L(n)] \end{cases}$$

where

$$E[W_{n+1}(X,D(n+1),S(n+1),L(n+1))|D(n),S(n),L(n)]=\sum Pr(D(n+1)|D(n)) \cdot$$
$$W_{n+1}(X,D(n+1),S(n+1)L(n+1)$$

---

*We are tacitly assuming that the relevant market is at least approximately competitive. Both major analyses of the tanker market, references 9 and 22, conclude that, with the exception of the short-lived tanker pool of the thirties, the tanker market represents one of the purer forms of competition found in real-world markets. The dry bulk market is institutionally quite similar. Operators in certain dry bulk markets feel that Japanese charterers cooperate in attempts to control rates. However, their recent withdrawal from the market at high rates can also be explained as speculation against inventory that the rates will drop, which speculation is perfectly consistent with a purely competitive market. However, in such cases, demand can no longer be assumed to be completely inelastic. The algorithm does not need this latter assumption except by way of convenience.

and $S(n+1)=S(n)+\Delta S(L(n))+\nabla S(S(n),R_1)$ where ΔS is the amount of launchings in ΔN consistent with the present order book and ∇S is the amount of scrappings and losses consistent with the present fleet size and charter rate. $L(n+1)=L(n)+\Delta L(L(n))$, $0(R_1,L(n))$ as before.

Notice that this formulation requires that the DM specify a distribution only over the future demand series and not over the rates. In general, future demand is a random variable about which the DM will have much more to go on. In effect, we have transferred the responsibility for simulating the market from the DM's internal processes to the algorithm leaving the DM only the extremely important function of cogitating about the future growth in demand for his services.

Continuing with the recursion relations, we have

$$W_n(0,D,S,L)=\max \begin{cases} B(n) \\ -C_L(n)+\rho E[W_{n+1}(-1,D(n+1),S(n+1),L(n+1))\,|\,D(n),S(n),L(n)] \\ -C_H(n)+\rho E[W_{n+1}(0,D(n+1),S(n+1),L(n+1))\,|\,D(n),S(n),L(n)] \\ R_m-C_m+\rho E[W_{n+1}(m-1,D(n+1),S(n+1),L(n+1))\,|\,D(n),S(n),L(n)] \end{cases}$$

and finally for the case where the ship is already on charter $W_n(k,D,S,L)=\rho E[(W_{n+1}(k-1,D(n+1),S(n+1),L(n+1))\,|\,D(n),S(n),L(n)]$ which holds for all k greater than 0 and less than M.

This algorithm has been programmed at M.I.T. and the results indicate that, for a moderately sized state space ($\Delta N=2$, M=25, ten D's, ten S's, ten L's), the cost of running the algorithm over a 25-year vessel life will be approximately \$250. This program is described in reference 21.

4.7 OVERALL FLEET POLICIES

As long as the owner is an EMV'er in a perfect capital market, as we have assumed, each of his ships can be treated as a separate entity, since by maximizing the expected net present value of each ship separately he will maximize the expected net present value from the fleet as a whole.* In such a situation, the industry dictum, "The vessel is the firm." holds. Thus, for the case of perfect liquidity and EMVing, we have already "solved" the multi-ship fleet owner's problem.

However, the limitations on this "solution" are indicated by the fact that, under these assumptions, the owner will employ all units of his charterable fleet in exactly the same manner. Cursory examination of the foregoing algorithms will reveal that if the owner decides to spot charter one of his charterable units he will spot charter all charterable units with the same general cost characteristics; likewise for long-term chartering. In actual fact, almost all independent owners choose to employ their fleet in a mixed manner--placing a portion in long-term charters, a portion in medium-term, and a portion in the voyage market. It is clear that either owners are risk-adverse or dealing in imperfect capital markets or both. If the evidence presented in Chapter 2 concerning Scandinavian owners' preference function is general, this mixing is more a product of capital market constraints than risk-aversion, for long-term charters can be mortgaged while short-term contracts cannot.

If we generalize the earlier solutions to incorporate either realistic financial markets or nonlinear preferences, the problem becomes computationally infeasible quite quickly. In both cases, the basic problem involves the fact that we can no longer consider each ship separately. The problem of the risk-adverse owner in a perfect capital market is quite similar to the problem faced by the combined charterer-owner such as the large oil company and this problem will be treated in the next section under that guise. For now, we will say what little we can about the EMV'er in an imperfect financial market.

---

*This statement once again assumes that the owner is facing a competitive market, that is, the manner in which he employs his ships does not affect the charter rates.

Given a description of such a market, it is no great trick to write down a dynamic program for solving this problem. Let us suppose, for example, as is sometimes the case, that an investor is limited in his borrowing by this current ratio. That is, financial institutions will lend him some multiple of his liquid or near-liquid assets but no more. Let D,S, and L be the market state variables as before. Let the vector $(X_1, X_2, X_3, \ldots, X_K)$ be the ship status variables for each of the present and potential ships in his fleet defined as before, except that $-3 \leq X_i \leq J$ implies the ith ship is presently on order and will be delivered $|X|-2$ voyage periods from now. $X_i = -2$ means the ith ship is neither in the fleet, nor on order. K is the maximum fleet size the owner wants to consider. Let C be the owner's liquid assets as defined by his bankers (but assumed independent of present market rates) and let F be his outstanding debt. Then, at any stage, the state of this owner is described by $(D,S,L,X_1,X_2,\ldots,X_K,C,F)$ and $W_n(D,S,L,X_1,X_2,\ldots X_K,C,F)$ is the corresponding expected present valued profits associated with this state. The owner's problem at any combination of stage and state is to maximize, over all possible vessel employment and fleet investment alternatives meeting the C/F limits, the difference between the present value of the revenues fixed by decisions made at this stage and the present value of the outlays fixed by decisions at this stage plus the discounted expected value of the W_{n+1} associated with the state which these decisions and Nature results in at the next stage. By now, it should be clear to the reader that writing down a recursion relation consistent with this statement presents no conceptual problems. It should be equally clear that such a dynamic program is computationally unthinkable for even a very small fleet size since the size of the state space grows exponentially with the number of ships in the fleet.

This impasse does not imply that such an owner can do no useful analysis but rather he can analyze only a small market of all fleet investment/vessel employment policies. An example of such limited analysis is given in the next section.

4.8 THE OWNER-CHARTERER'S PROBLEM

The obverse of the EMV-imperfect financial market problem
is the non-EMV-perfect capital market problem. The latter problem is approximately the situation faced by the large-scale
shipper-owner such as the international oil companies which
dominate the buyer side of the tanker market. Generally, these
organizations have practically unlimited borrowing power. Thus,
by our earlier argument, their observed behavior of owning something like 40% of their transportation requirements, term chartering about 40% more and voyage chartering the rest can be explained only in terms of risk-adversion.

Generally speaking, the risk-adverse fleet operator's problem is no easier to solve than the EMVer-imperfect capital
market problem since once again the state space is astronomi-
cally large. In the case of the owner-charterer we need as
state variables the length of time each of the chartered and
owned ships presently under control will be under his control
as well as the state-of-the-market variables and the variable(s)
upon which his preference function is based.* This is clearly
a computationally infeasible situation.

A modicum of progress can be made if we restrict our attention to a very small set of strategies: the fixed fleet mix
policies. A fixed fleet mix policy is a policy in which the
owner-charterer attempts to maintain fixed proportions of his
requirements in each of several categories. For simplicity,
let us assume three such categories: owned, five-year charters,
and single-voyage charters. Such a policy can be characterized
by only three variables: X_o, X_5, X_s where X_o is the percent of
transport which is obtained through five-year charters and
X_s is percent of transport which is obtained in the voyage

---

*In a perfect capital market, it is reasonable to assume that
 corporate preference is based on present valued transportation costs.

market. Fixed fleet mix policies are not a particularly brilliant subset of strategies. For one thing, they do not vary with the current state of the market. However, such policies form at least general guidelines for many real-world owner-charterers and as long as you are going to follow such a policy you might as well pick the best of such policies. Thus, this set of policies is of some interest.

Since the above-outlined three-category fixed fleet mix policy has only two independent variables, it is a reasonably simple matter to find that three-category fixed fleet mix policy which maximizes expected preference by straightforward enumeration. That is, we first might test, say, the policy $(X_O=1.00, X_5=0, X_S=0)$, then the policy $(X_O=.90, X_5=.10, X_S=0)$, etc., sequentially adjusting the fleet mix until we arrive at the policy $(X_O=0, X_5=0, X_S=1.00)$. In other words, if we can find a means of obtaining the expected preference associated with the present valued transportation costs which results from a particular fleet mix policy, we can determine the best of these policies by simply repeating the calculations for each of these policies.

One can obtain an estimate of the expected preference associated with a particular fleet mix policy by straightforward Monte Carlo simulation if one is willing to assume:

1) The owner-charterer will review his transportation requirements on a periodic basis, say, by quarters. Let n denote the nth such quarter.

2) The DM is willing to specify a cut-off date to the problem: that is, he is willing to cost out his policy for the next, say, twenty years and ignore what happens afterwards. Let N be the cut-off date in quarters.

3) The DM is willing to assume a dynamic model of the charter market such as the supply-and-demand-based model described earlier. For this application, however, there is no limitation on the number of state variables or the number of values that any state

136

variable can assume. Therefore, a very detailed model of the market can be used. The DM must be willing to specify distributions on any random variables in this model.

4)   The DM is willing to describe his in-house transportation requirements $\{d_n:n=1,2,\ldots N\}$ in ton-miles per quarter through the future. The d_n's may either be deterministic or random variables. In the latter case he must be willing to specify distributions on these random variables. The distribution on d_n may depend in any manner whatsoever on past d_n's and the present and past values of the market variables. Generally, if industrywide demand increases due to, say, the Suez Canal closing, then in-house demand will also increase.

Given all these assumptions, one can test a particular fixed fleet mix policy by straightforward Monte Carlo simulation. Suppose we wish to test the $(X_o=.40, X_5=.40, X_s=.20)$ policy, then we would start our model of the market off, using the present actual values of the state variables, generate the values of the state variables at the next quarter, using the model's relations and a random number generator to obtain samples of the random variables, and then repeat the process for the following quarter and so on until n=N. Concurrent with this simulation we would keep track of the in-house transportation requirements and the status of the in-house transportation commitments and adjust these commitments as required to maintain the percentages specified by the policy presently under consideration. The simulation keeps track of the present valued costs and revenues associated with the resulting purchase and sales. The result at n=N is a sample of the total present valued costs associated with the policy for the period n=0 to n=N.

This simulation has to be repeated a number of times to obtain a histogram of the associated total costs. After one

137

has made enough runs so that one is satisfied that the resulting histogram is a reasonable approximation of the distribution of costs associated with the policy,* then one applies one's preference function of outcomes and takes the expectation. One then repeats the whole process for another fixed fleet mix policy and so on.

---

*The problem of when to stop rerunning is a Bayesian decision theory problem in its own right which we won't go into. In general, a single run will be quite fast since one is merely simulating a single specific trajectory of the process. Thus a set of, say, 1,000 runs is computationally feasible, especially if one keeps track of more than one policy on a given run.

CHAPTER 5

MAINTENANCE AND REPLACEMENT--PROBLEMS IN WHICH THE PROBABILITIES CHANGE

In this chapter we turn our attention to an interesting set of decisions which arise in the maintenance and repair of marine systems. The marine environment is harsh and changeable and the costs of failure can be quite high due to the value of the systems and their relative isolation. Thus, the balancing of redundancy and conservative design, preventive maintenance and replacement against possible failures is a critical issue in many marine situations. Such problems involve two levels of uncertainties.

a) Even if one knows how "good" or reliable a particular system is, one cannot predict with certainty when it will fail or how often it will fail in a particular period;

b) Often one doesn't know how reliable a system is, for one has had experience with only a small sample of the system in question.

Thus, a related problem is determining how "good" a system is from a small set of failure data. We will begin our study of such problems by examining a situation in which these two sets of uncertainties are related in an extremely well-structured manner and then move to the more general problem of constructing maintenance and overhaul strategies for equipment about which one has only a limited amount of failure data.

5.1 THE BOILER TUBE PULLING PROBLEM

The biggest single job in the overhaul of marine steam turbine machinery is usually the inspection and repair of boiler tubes. In general, not all and sometimes very few of the 1,200 or so tubes in a boiler need replacement. However, one cannot determine for certain whether a tube needs replacement without going through the laborious and expensive process of pulling it. On the other hand, failure to replace a defective tube can lead to substantial loss of power, and expensive shutdowns, perhaps at critical moments in the ship's career. Finally, the best information one has on the likelihood of the condition of the remaining tubes in the boiler is the condition of the tubes already pulled. The problem thus arises: how many tubes should we pull and how should we change this decision as the state of the tubes already pulled becomes known to us?

In order to get started on this problem, consider the following idealized boiler. The boiler has N tubes. A tube is either defective or not defective--there are no in-betweens. More discriminating models are possible which distinguish between, say, a failed tube, a badly corroded tube, a lightly corroded tube, and a perfect tube at some expense in computational feasibility. For now, we stick to the binary case.

Let p be the probability that a tube is defective. If the DM is willing to assume that all tubes face approximately the same conditions, then it is reasonable for him to assume that one tube is as likely to be defective as another--that is, all tubes have the same p. Unfortunately, the yard will not know exactly what these conditions were. Therefore, p cannot be known with certainty. In fact, our job is to attempt to estimate p from the conditions of the tubes already pulled. Roughly: if a lot of the tubes are bad, then it is more likely that p is close to 1.00 and thus more likely that the next tube(s) to be pulled are defective. Bayesian decision theory will allow us to make these intuitive feelings operative in a systematic way.

In actual fact, not all the tubes in a boiler face similar conditions with respect to corrosion. The different segments of the boiler--the economizer, the steam generator and the superheater--face very different fireside and steam conditions and, in fact, different corrosive mechanisms apply to the different parts of the boiler. The above assumption can be extended to cover some of these differences by regarding the economizer, steam generator and superheater as each a separate "boiler" with its own p.

With this caveat, let C(m) be the cost associated with pulling and replacing m tubes in a block. This should be the additional cost, given that the boiler is open and under repair. In general, C(m) will not be linear in m, reflecting economies due to pulling tubes in a block. Let F(k) be the expected cost of not fixing k tubes which are defective. These costs should include the cost of downtime, of plugging, and of the resultant loss in power. The estimation of these costs is a problem in uncertainty in itself. For now, assume we have somehow ascertained F(k).

In elementary probability courses, it is demonstrated that if p is the probability of a defective tube on a single trial then, if we pull m tubes in a block, the probability of k of those tubes being defective is

$$\frac{m!}{k! \ (m-k)!} \ p^k (1-p)^{m-k}$$

This function is called the Bernoulli density function and denoted $f_\beta(k|p,m)$. Unfortunately, we don't know what p is and further, as the results of our earlier investigations of the boiler become clear, presumably our ideas about p will change. As Bayesians, if p is a variable about which we are uncertain, then by introspection we can obtain the subjective probability that p takes on each of its possible values.* This set of probabilities is called the subjective distribution of p. What can be said about this distribution?

Well, since p is a probability, it must be between 0.0 and 1.0 inclusive. To get our thinking started, let's say before pulling any tubes, the DM believes that one possible value of

---

*It may help our thinking to regard p as the probability with which Nature picks a defective tube. However, we don't know what Nature's probability is. In general, therefore, our probability that the next tube is defective will not equal p.

p between 0 and 1 is as likely as any other. That is, when the
DM is asked at what canonical chance π he would be indifferent
between a lottery which yields him a valuable prize with canonical chance π and a lottery which yields him the same valuable
prize if p is less than x, the DM says π = x and he says this
for all possible x between 0 and 1. That is, the DM answers to
this set of questions lie along the straight line in Figure 5.1.
This straight line is called the DM's *subjective distribution*
on the random variable p. The derivative of this function is
shown in Figure 5.2. The derivative of a distribution function
is called a *density function*. In this case, the density function is simply a straight line of value 1.00 between 0 and 1.
This particular density function has been unimaginatively tagged
the uniform density function. In general, a density function
is as good a measure of the probability of the various values
of a random variable as a distribution function. The advantages
of working with density functions will become clear as we
proceed.

An analytic representation of the uniform density function
can be obtained by using the Beta density function $f_\beta(p|r',n')$
where the parameters r' and n' equal 1 and 2 respectively. In
general, the family of Beta densities is given by

$$f_\beta(p|r',n') = \frac{1}{B(r',n')} \, p^{r'-1} \, (1-p)^{n'-r'-1}$$

$$p < 1$$
$$r,n > 0$$

where $B(r',n')$, the complete Beta integral is given by

$$B(r',n') = \int_0^1 x^{r'-1} (1-x)^{n'-r'-1} \, dx = \frac{(r'-1)!\,(n'-r'-1)!^*}{(n-1)!}$$

The Beta density functions are positive only between 0 and 1 and
by varying the parameters r' and n' a quite rich family of

---

*Throughout this book the factorial notation is taken in its
 generalized sense, i.e., $(x-1)! = \Gamma(x)$ and thus is defined
 for all x greater than 0.

142

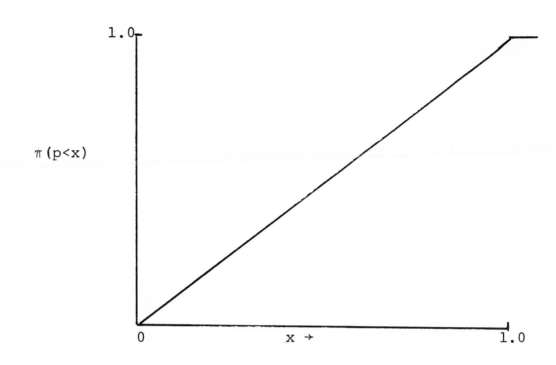

FIGURE 5-1   DM's Distribution on p

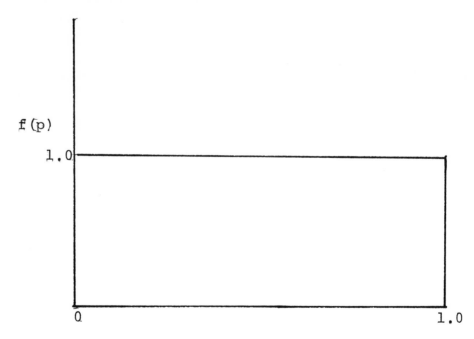

FIGURE 5-2   DM's Density Function on p

143

distributions can be obtained. Almost any smooth unimodal and
some bimodal density functions on the interval [0,1] can be
closely approximated by a Beta density. Some members of this
family are shown in Figure 5-3. Notice that substituting r'=1
and n'=2 yields the uniform density.

Given this ability to approximate a wide range of possible
distributions on our unknown likelihood of a defective tube, p,
the DM will lose little generality if he decides to limit himself to Beta densities in choosing a subjective distribution on
p. This essentially harmless limitation has some very significant analytical advantages.

First, given that one approximates one's subjective distri-
bution on p by a member of the Beta family $f_\beta(p|r',n')$ one can
obtain a closed form expression for the probability that one
will obtain k defective tubes if one starts the process by pulling m tubes in a block. For, by the Sum Rule, the probability of k bad tubes out of m given Beta density on p with parameters r' and n' is equal to the sum over all p of the product
of the probability of k conditional on p and the probability of
p. Or

$$Pr(k|r',n',m) = \int_0^1 f_\beta(k|p,m) \cdot f_\beta(p|r',n')\,dp$$

This is simply a straightforward application of the Sum Rule,
the only difference being that since p can take on a continuum
of values we have to use integration rather than summation.
Substituting into the above expression, we have

$$= \int_0^1 \frac{m!}{k!(m-k)!} p^k (1-p)^{m-k} \frac{\cdot 1}{B(r',n')} \cdot p^{r'-1} (1-p)^{n'-r'-1}\,dp$$

$$= \frac{m!(n'-1)!}{k!(m-k)!(r'-1)!(n'-r'-1)!} \int_0^1 p^{r'+k-1}(1-p)^{(n'+m)-(r'+k)-1}\,dp$$

$$= \frac{m!(n'-1)!(r'+k-1)!(n'+m-r'-k-1)!}{k!(m-k)!(r'-1)!(n'-r'-1)!(n'+m-1)!}$$

$$= \binom{m}{k} \frac{B(r'+k,n'+m)}{(r',n')}$$

144

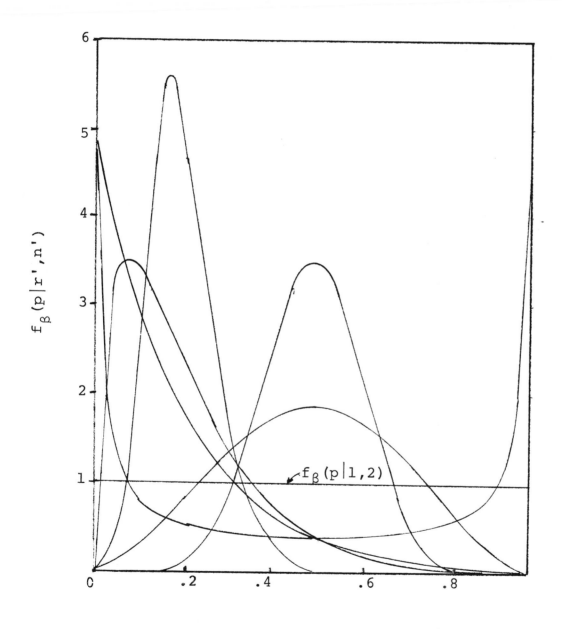

FIGURE 5.3   A FEW BETA DENSITY FUNCTIONS

145

This density function is called the Betabinomial and is denoted by

$$f_{\beta B}(k \mid r', n', m).$$

The second and more important reason for choosing to approximate the subjective distribution on p by a Beta involves the updating of this distribution as a result of having observed, say, r defective tubes in the first n pulled. After having obtained this result, the Bayesian DM's new feelings about p will be given by the conditional probability on p given r defective out of n and his original distribution on p which is characterized by the parameters r' and n'. Let us denote this conditional probability by $f(p \mid r; n, r'n')$. By Bayes Rule,

$$f(p \mid r, n'r', n') = \frac{Pr(r \mid p, n; r', n') \cdot Pr(p \mid n; r', n')}{\int_0^1 Pr(r \mid p, n'r', n') \cdot Pr(p \mid n; r', n') dp}$$

where integration replaces summation since p is continuous. Now, given a particular p the probability of r defective in n trial is

$$\binom{r}{n} p^r (1-p)^{n-r}$$

regardless of r' and n'. Similarly, the number of trials n by itself cannot tell us anything about p. Hence,

$$Pr(p \mid n'r', n') = Pr(p \mid r', n') = f_\beta(p \mid r', n')$$

Thus,

$$f(p \mid r, n; r', n') = \frac{\binom{r}{n} p^r (1-p)^{n-r} \frac{1}{B(r'n')} \cdot p^{r'-1} (1-p)^{n'-r'-1}}{\int_0^1 \binom{r}{n} p^r (1-p)^{n-r} \frac{1}{B(r', n')} p^{r'-1} (1-p)^{n'-r'-1} dp}$$

$$= \frac{p^{r+r'-1} (1-p)^{(n+n')-(r+r')-1}}{\int_0^1 p^{r+r'-1} (1-p)^{n+n')-(r+r')-1} dp}$$

146

$$= \frac{p^{r+r'-1}(1-p)^{(n+n')-(r+r')-1}}{B(r+r',n+n')}$$

$$= f_\beta(p|r+r',n+n')$$

Thus, if we choose to approximate our subjective distribution on p by a Beta where p is the parameter of Bernoulli process, then our distribution on p *after* having observed a sample of r defectives in n trials is also a Beta. Further, the parameters of the Beta we start with, which we will call the *prior*, and the Beta we end up with, which we will call the *posterior*, are related in an extremely simple manner. In fact, if we denote the new parameters by r" and n" then r" = r+r' and n"=n+n'. Thus, by a clever choice of the form of our prior we don't even have to do the Bayes Rule computations after having observed a sample, but rather can write down the new distribution on p immediatly. A prior which has this property is called a *conjugate prior*. What we have shown is that the Beta density function is the conjugate prior to the Bernoulli density. To illustrate how this works, suppose the DM had started off with the wishy-washy uniform prior described above, that is, r'=1 and n'=2, and suppose he chose to pull 20 tubes and observed that 5 of them were defective. His new feelings about p then are described by the Beta with parameters r"=5+1 and n"=20+2. This new density function is shown alongside his original function in Figure 5-4. As might be expected, the DM now more heavily weights p's near 1/4 and also his new distribution is considerably tighter than the old, reflecting his increase in knowledge about p. In fact, the DM now has some very definite feelings about p. He is almost dead sure that p is less than 0.5, and if you asked him at what π he would be indifferent between a lottery awarding him a valuable prize with canonical chance π and a lottery awarding him the same prize if p is between 0.1 and 0.4, he would answer, "I prefer the lottery based on p for any π's less than 0.9." Quite a change from the π=0.3 he started out with.

Let us suppose, after having observed 5 defective out of

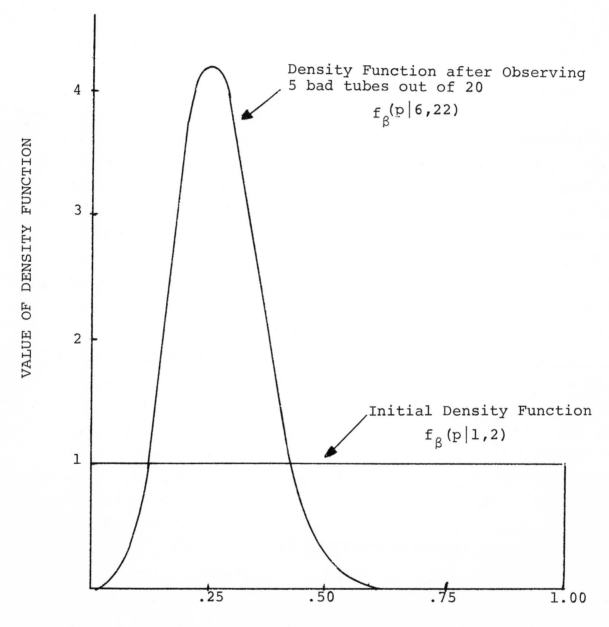

VALUE OF NATURE'S PROBABILITY, p

FIGURE 5.4

PRIOR AND POSTERIOR DENSITIES ON p

148

20, the DM decides to pull 8 more tubes and observes 3 of them to be defective. What is his new distribution on p? Well, clearly the distribution he should start out with is his "old" posterior, $f_\beta(p|6,22)$ which becomes his new prior, since it represents his state of knowledge prior to the most recent results. His new posterior, his distribution of p after the second set of pullings, is by the above expressions a Beta with parameters 3+6 and 8+22. *In short, the posterior distribution for one set of results becomes the prior for the next.*

It should be also clear that as long as the parameters of the original prior are small (i.e., the original subjective distribution is wishy-washy) it will not be long before $r''\tilde{=}r$ and $n''\tilde{=}n$. That is, the data will overwhelm the DM's original feelings.* A choice of original parameters r' and n' is equivalent to saying: my prior feelings before commencing any tests are the same as if I had observed r' defective in n' tests and nothing else. Thus, it doesn't make much difference what original distribution we start off with as long as it is wishy-washy. In fact, if one wanted to give prior feelings no weight at all, one could make r'=0 and n'=0.

Finally, by a straightforward generalization of the earlier argument leading to the Betabinomial, the probability of observing k defective tubes out of a batch of m pulled after DM has already pulled n tubes and r of these were defective is simply the Betabinomial whose parameters are the parameters of the present distribution on p, and m: $f_{\beta B}(k|r+r',n+n',m))$.

---

*If the DM does have strong feelings (say, he is sure p is near 1), he should pick an original distribution which is consistent with these feelings and his results will be affected accordingly. In general, the prior will depend on a preliminary inspection of the tube bank and the general condition of the boiler.

5.2 AN ALGORITHM FOR DETERMINING THE OPTIMAL TUBE PULLING POLICY, GIVEN THE FOREGOING PROBABILISTIC CONSIDERATIONS

We have developed all the probabilistic considerations relevant to this problem. We now proceed to the development of a dynamic program for determining minimal expected cost tube pulling strategies--strategies which, since they realize the probabilities can and will change as we move through the process, properly weight the value of experimentation.

At any point in the tube pulling process, the current situation can be described by the pair (n,r) where n is the number of tubes already pulled and r is the number of these tubes which have turned out to be defective. n is the stage variable and r is the state variable for this process. We define an optimal value function $W_n(r)$ over all possible combinations of n and r to be the minimum attainable expected cost associated with any further tube pulling and any defective tubes left unrepaired, given that we have already pulled n tubes r of which were defective. As usual, we proceed to develop a recursive relationship on $W_n(r)$.

At any point (n,r) in the process, we have the following alternatives:

1) We can stop pulling tubes, close up the boiler, and bear the expected costs associated with any defective tubes we have failed to repair.

2) We can pull m tubes $0 < m \leq N-n$ and pay the cost, C(m), associated with this job and then see where we are.

Let us develop the minimum expected costs associated with each of these alternatives. Assuming there are N tubes in the boiler and we have already pulled n of these and have observed r defective, by the foregoing arguments the probability that k of the remaining N-n tubes are bad is $f_{\beta B}(k|r+r',n+n',N-n)$. Thus, the expected future costs of not pulling any more tubes after having observed r defective out of n is:

$$\sum_{k=0}^{N-n} f_{\beta B}(k|r+r',n+n',N-n) F(k)$$

150

where F(k) is the expected cost associated with k non-repaired defective tubes.

If after having observed r bad tubes out of n pulled we decide to keep pulling, the situation is a little more complicated. Suppose we decide to pull m tubes and see where we are. Well, we will certainly bear the costs of pulling and replacing m tubes, (m). Out of the m tubes pulled, k will be defective where k is a random variable between 0 and m inclusive. We already know what the density function on k is. It is $f_{\beta B}(k|r+r', n+n', m)$. After we have pulled m tubes and k of them turned out to be defective, we will be faced with the original choice, only now we will have pulled n+m tubes and will have observed r+k defective. But the minimum cost attainable from this latter situation forward is by definition $W_{n+m}(r+k)$. In short, the minimum expected n+m cost associated with the alternative of pulling m>0 tubes after having pulled n and observed r defective is

$$C(m) + \sum_{k=0}^{m} f_{\beta B}(k|r+r', n+n', m) \cdot W_{n+n}(k) \quad .$$

But after having pulled n tubes and observed r failures, we will want to follow the expected cost-minimizing alternative. Moreover, the value of that alternative will be $W_n(r)$ or

$$W_n(r) = \min_{0 \leq m \leq N-n} \begin{cases} \sum_{k=0}^{M-n} f_{\beta B}(k|r+r', n+n', N-n) \cdot F(k) \\ \\ C(m) + \sum_{k=0}^{m} f_{\beta B}(k|r+r', n+n', m) \cdot W_{n+m}(k) \end{cases}$$

Thus, this formulation leads to a computational simple dynamic program.* However, there are two things to note about this program, one unimportant and one important. The unimportant feature of this program is that, unlike the earlier dynamic programs, the value of the stage variable at the next decision

---

*A computer program for implementing this algorithm is available from the M.I.T. Department of Ocean Engineering.

is a function of the present decision. Thus, this algorithm involves a slight but obvious generalization of our concept of stage. The reader should review the basic recursive reasoning of dynamic programming and note that it does not require that all decisions at any particular stage lead to the same stage.

The important thing to note about this program is that, unlike any of the earlier ones, it is truly adaptive in that it accounts for the fact that not only will our earlier decisions place us in some state from which we want to do the best we can; but also that, as a result of our earlier decisions and the results, we will have learned something about the probabilities underlying our problem. Further, in calculating the optimal value table it will weight the chances of future learning and the value to be obtained from this learning in deciding what to do. In short, this dynamic program properly weights the value of experimentation in the same manner that we weighted the value of experimentation in Joe's problem.

5.3 USING SMALL SAMPLE FAILURE DATA IN DETERMINING MAINTENANCE AND REPLACEMENT POLICIES

We now wish to turn to a more general set of problems involving preventive maintenance. As noted earlier, these problems involve two sets of uncertainties:

a) Even if one knows how reliable a system is--that is, if one is absolutely sure of the probabilities of failure--the timing and number of failures which will actually occur cannot be known by the DM before the fact;

b) Generally, the DM is not only not sure of the relevant probabilities of failures, but often he has only the sketchiest data upon which to base his feelings about these probabilities.

Classical reliability theory has tended to ignore the second set of uncertainties. For example, in many situations one can assume that the probability of failure of a component in the

152

next time increment does not depend on how long the component has been operating. Properly stated, this assumption implies that the probability of r such failures in a time interval T is given by

$$Pr(r|T,\lambda) = \frac{e^{-\lambda T} (\lambda T)^r}{r!}$$

which function is known as the Poisson density function and denoted $f_p(r|T,\lambda)$.* Under this assumption, the parameter λ, known as the *mean failure rate* of the component, becomes the sole descriptor of a system's reliability characteristics. Yet, classical reliability offers almost no advice about how to determine λ. The engineer is forced to skirt the problem by such ad hoc procedures as assuming that the average failure rate observed in his usually small sample is the mean failure rate of the component in question. This leads to such absurdities as a zero mean failure rate for those subsystems for which he has yet to observe a failure, and a general feeling of discomfort in applying the whole reliability theory apparatus. Using such assumptions, one ends up with the same probability of failure in, say, a year's operation whether one observes one failure in two years of operation or twenty failures in forty years of operation. The maintenance man understandably feels that the size of his sample should be reflected in the probabilities he generates.

The Bayesian views such physical parameters as a mean failure rate on which we have limited data as a quantity we cannot be sure about, in other words, as a random variable. He uses whatever data exists on such a parameter--whether it be a very small sample or a large one--to develop distributions on such variables. As more data becomes available, these distributions are updated and tightened according to Bayes Rule to reflect his increased knowledge about the parameter. From the

---

*Derivations of the Poisson density function can be found in any elementary probability text. See, for example, reference 4, Chapter 4.

current distributions on such parameters, all the usual probabilities of reliability theory can be computed by straightforward, if sometimes tedious, application of probability theory in the same manner that we were able to compute the probability that k of the next m boiler tubes would be defective once we had the present distribution on the physical parameter p in the last section.

Surprisingly enough, taking this viewpoint will often reduce the data reduction and updating problem, since all our present knowledge about a particular quantity (say, mean failure rate of a certain gas turbine) is summed up in its present distribution and, as new data becomes available, this distribution changes in a simple mechanical manner. This is especially true if we choose the form of our distributions on the unknown parameters in a judicious manner, as will be illustrated below.

5.4 A BAYESIAN MODEL FOR ANALYZING AGE-DEPENDENT FAILURE DATA

Assuming that failures are distributed according to the Poisson density function for the entire life of a subsystem is not a very interesting exercise, since if the probability of failures does not increase with age then there is never any point in replacing a component before it fails. Under this assumption, there is no point in preventive replacement.

A more general hypothesis is to assume that the failures are distributed according to a Poisson distribution in which the mean failure rate depends on the age of the system. An approximation to this hypothesis is to assume that the mean failure rate is constant in any year of the life of the system, m, but can change from year to year.

Under this latter assumption, if r_m is the number of failures in year m of the life of the subsystem and λ_m is the mean rate of failure of the subsystem in year m, then

$$\Pr(r_m | \lambda_m) = \frac{e^{-\lambda_m}(\lambda_m)^{r_m}}{r_m!} \ .$$

154

Of course, the DM has no way of knowing with certainty what the λ_m's m=1,2,... are. Hence, we take a Bayesian view and postulate a prior distribution on each λ_m. As before, we will choose our prior from a family of functions the form of which family results in a great simplification of the Bayes Rule calculations. For the Poisson density function such as family of priors is the Gamma density function. The Gamma densities are a two-parameter family given by

$$f_\gamma(\lambda_m | r'_m t'_m) = \frac{e^{-\lambda_m t'_m}(\lambda_m t'_m)^{r'_m - 1} t'_m}{(r'_m - 1)!} \qquad \lambda_m \geq 0$$

This is a remarkably rich family of functions, some of whose members are shown in Figure 5.5. Almost any unimodal density function over the interval $[0,\infty]$ can be at least roughly approximately by a Gamma.

If one chooses a Gamma prior with parameters r'_m and t'_m on the mean failure rate of a component at age m and then observes r_m failures of this component in t_m years of operation at age m, then by Bayes Rule the posterior distribution on λ_m is given by:

$$f(\lambda_m | R'_m, t'_m, r_m, t_m) = \frac{\dfrac{e^{-\lambda_m t_m}(\lambda_m t_m)^{r_m} e^{-\lambda_m t'_m}(\lambda_m t'_m)^{r'_m - 1} \cdot t'_m}{r_m!(r'_m - 1)!}}{\displaystyle\int_0^\infty \frac{e^{-\lambda_m t_m}(\lambda_m t_m)^{r_m} e^{-\lambda_m t'_m}(\lambda_m t'_m)^{r'_m - 1} \cdot t'_m \, d\lambda_m}{r_m!(r'_m-1)!}}$$

$$= \frac{\dfrac{e^{-\lambda_m(t_m+t'_m)} \lambda_m^{r_m+r'_m-1} \cdot t_m^{r_m} t_m'^{r'_m}}{r_m!(r'_m-1)!}}{\displaystyle\int_0^\infty \frac{e^{-\lambda_m(t_m+t'_m)} \lambda^{r_m+r'_m-1} \cdot t_m^{r_m} t_m'^{r'_m} \, d\lambda_m}{r_m!(r'_m-1)!}}$$

155

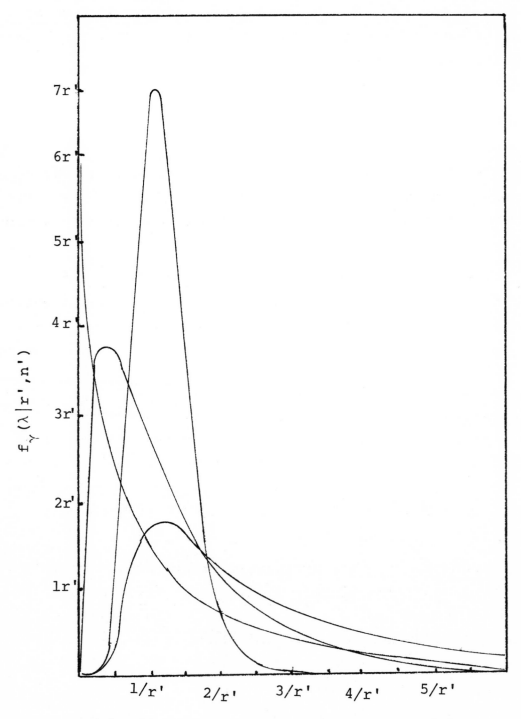

FIGURE 5.5   A FEW GAMMA DENSITY FUNCTIONS

156

$$= \frac{\dfrac{t_m^{r_m} t_m'^{r_m'}}{r_m!(r_m'-1)!} \cdot e^{-\lambda_m(t_m+t_m')} \lambda_m^{r_m+r_m'-1}}{\dfrac{t_m^{r_m} t_m'^{r_m'}}{r_m!(r_m'-1)!} \displaystyle\int_0^\infty e^{-\lambda_m(t_m+t_m')} \lambda_m^{t_m+r_m'-1}\, d\lambda_m}$$

$$= \frac{\dfrac{t_m^{r_m} t_m'^{t_m'}}{r_m!(r_m'-1)!} \; e^{-\lambda_m(t_m+t_m')} \lambda_m^{r_m+r_m'-1}}{\dfrac{t_m^{r_m} t_m'^{r_m'}}{r_m!(r_m'-1)!} \; \dfrac{(r_m+r_m'-1)!}{(t_m+t_m')^{r_m+r_m'}}}$$

Cancelling out,

$$= \frac{e^{-\lambda_m(t_m+t_m')} (\lambda_m(t_m+t_m'))^{r_m+r_m'}(t_m+t_m')}{(r_m+r_m'-1)!}$$

$$= f_\gamma(\lambda_m \mid r_m+r_m', t_m+t_m')$$

That is, if we start with a Gamma prior with parameters r_m' and t_m' the posterior distribution on the mean failure rate of the component at age m after observing r_m failures in t_m years of operation of the system at this age is also a Gamma whose parameters are r_m+t_m' and t_m+t_m'. Once again we can circumvent the Bayes Rule computations. The Gamma family is the conjugate prior to the Poisson density.

The denominator in the above expressions before cancellation is the probability of both r_m and λ_m summed over all λ_m. According to the Sum Rule, it is simply the probability of r_m failures in t_m years of operation at age m if the parameters of the present distribution on λ_m are r_m' and t_m'. This density function which we will denote

$$f_{nB}(r_m \mid r_m', t_m', t_m)$$

is called the negative binomial. It corresponds to the Beta binomial in the tube pulling problem.

5.5 A SIMPLE EXAMPLE OF HOW THE FAILURE DATA ANALYSIS WOULD PROCEED

The above description of the methodology for obtaining the distributions on the number of failures and the loss per failure makes the analysis appear more complicated than it actually is. To illustrate this, consider the following example. Let us suppose from the data we find that there have been 10 failures of the component in question in year 4 of the life of this component in 40 ship years of operation of the component when it was 4 years old. We wish to determine the distribution on the number of this type of failure in year 4 of the life of the subsystem which is consistent with this data. To start out we need an original prior on the mean failure rate, λ_4. Now, before analyzing the data, we don't know very much about λ_4 other than its positive and it probably isn't very large. To describe these wishy-washy feelings we need a correspondingly indefinite prior--one where λ_4 is about as likely to be one number as another. Suppose we choose a Gamma distribution with parameters $r_4' = .05$ and $t_4' = .1$, that is

$$\Pr(\lambda_4) = \frac{e^{-.1\lambda_4} \cdot (.1\lambda_4)^{-.95}}{\Gamma(.05)}$$

This distribution is shown in Figure 5.6. Its breadth and lack of well-defined peaks indicates that at this point we are quite unsure about the value of λ_4. The probability density function on the number of failures in a year consistent with this distribution is shown in Figure 5.7. It is

$$f_{nB}(r_4 \mid .05, .10, 1)$$

Now, the advantage of choosing a Gamma prior is that our distribution on m_4 after having observed the data can be ob-

158

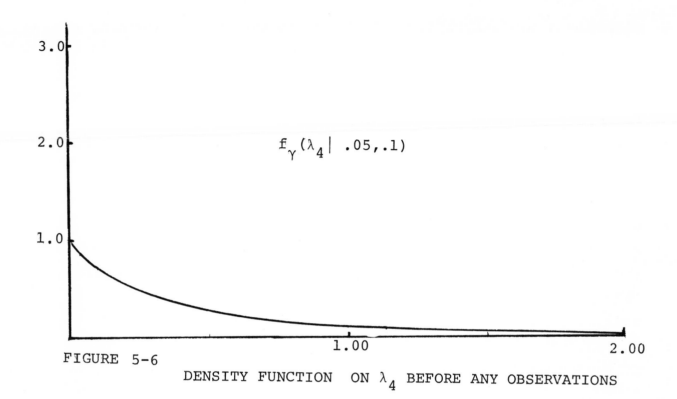

FIGURE 5-6

DENSITY FUNCTION ON λ_4 BEFORE ANY OBSERVATIONS

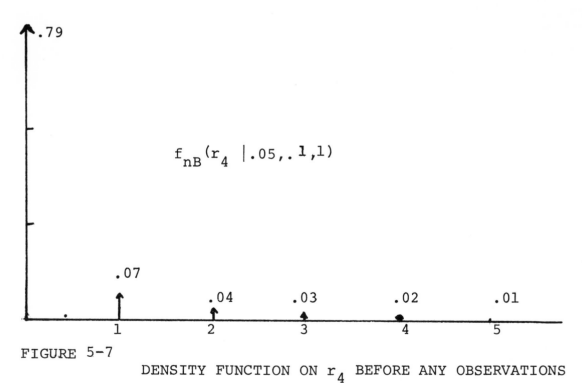

FIGURE 5-7

DENSITY FUNCTION ON r_4 BEFORE ANY OBSERVATIONS

tained by simple combination of the parameters of the prior and the data. In fact we have seen that if r_4' is the number of failures observed in t_4 years, the conditional distribution on λ_4 given the data is a Gamma whose parameters r'' and t'' are simply:

$$r_4'' = r_4 + r_4' \qquad t_4'' = t_4 + t_4'$$

Thus, given, say, $r_4 = 10$ failures in $t_4 = 40$ ship years, then the distribution on λ_4 after analysis of the data is a Gamma with parameters $r_4'' = 10 + .05 = 10.05$ and $t_4'' = 40 + 1 + 40.1$. This distribution is sketched in Figure 5.8.

Clearly this second distribution is almost wholly a product of the data, as it should be, since our earlier feelings on λ_4 were so wishy-washy. In short, for any wishy-washy prior (small r', small t') and any significant amount of data essentially the same posterior distribution will be obtained.* Of course, if we did have strong prior feelings about λ_4 for some reason, we would pick a tighter prior and, as it should, the posterior would be less affected by the data.

Of course, our real goal is not a distribution on λ_4, the unknown mean failure rate, but rather the distribution on the number of failures. As noted earlier, the new distribution on r_4, the number of failures in a year, is

$$f_{nB}(r_4 \mid 10.05, 40.1, 1) = \frac{1^{r_4} \cdot 40.1^{10.05}}{r_4! \; 9.05!} \frac{(9.05 + r_4)!}{(41.1)^{10.05 + r_4}}$$

---

*In fact, by making r' = 0, t' = 0 the posterior distribution will be wholly a function of the data. Of course, r' = 0, t' = 0 does not represent any real distribution, although it can be thought of as that distribution which given equal probability (0) to all points between 0 and ∞. From this point of view, the original prior becomes merely a gedanken-experiment to get our thinking (and our analysis) started.

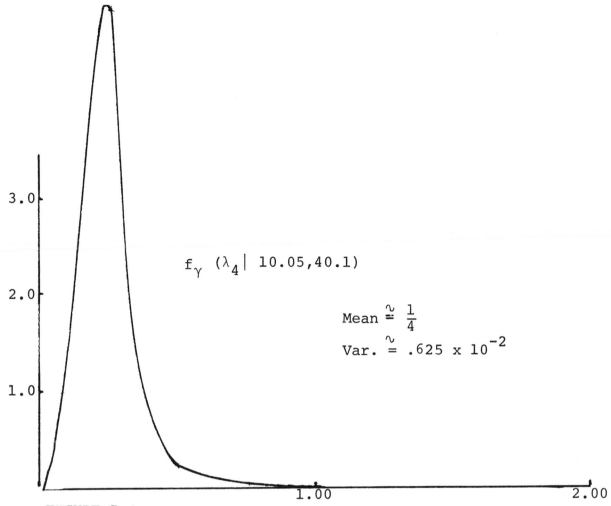

$$f_\gamma \ (\lambda_4 \mid \ 10.05, 40.1)$$

Mean $\cong \dfrac{1}{4}$

Var. $\cong .625 \times 10^{-2}$

FIGURE 5.8   DENSITY FUNCTION ON   AFTER OBSERVING 10 FAILURES
IN 40 SHIP YEARS OF OPERATION

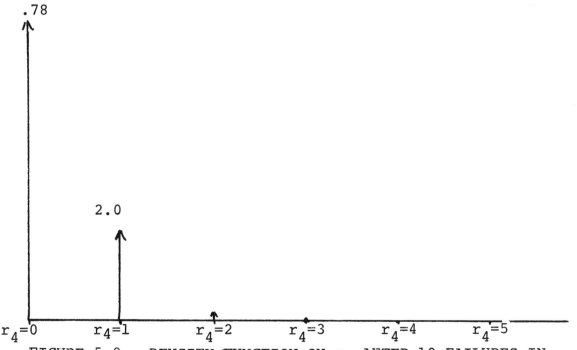

FIGURE 5.9   DENSITY FUNCTION ON r_4 AFTER 10 FAILURES IN
40 SHIP YEARS OF OPERATION

161

This distribution is sketched in Figure 5.9. Thus, we see that our rather long-winded discussion leads to a simple algebraic determination of the distribution of r_4 from the raw data.

Furthermore, updating with new information is even simpler. Suppose that a year later we have observed one more failure in 4 ship years of operations of 4-year-old components. How should we change the distribution on r_4? Well, the old distribution on λ_4, f_λ $(\lambda_4 | 10.05, 40.1)$ becomes our new prior and $r_4 = 1$ and $t_4 = 4$. Thus, the updated distribution on λ_4 is

$$f_\lambda (\lambda_4 | 10.05 + 1, 40.1 + 4)$$

and the corresponding distribution for r_4 is

$$f_{nB} (r_4 | 11.05, 44.1, 1) \quad .$$

Thus, updating the distributions as a result of new data is simplicity itself. These updated distributions are shown in Figures 5.10 and 5.11. In short, by properly choosing our priors on the unknown parameters, raw failure and cost of failure data can quite easily be transformed into the relevant distributions, and, further, these distributions can be updated in a simple and natural way as new data becomes available without recourse to the original data.

5.6 THE AUTOMATIC REPLACEMENT LIST

As a simple example of how this thinking might be employed, consider the situation facing a fleet operator or a military commander who has a sizable number of ships coming in for overhaul at regular intervals. One of the decisions which he faces is, which items of equipment should be replaced even though they have not yet failed or even exhibited particularly unfavorable symptoms? Now in the last section, we have seen that if the DM is willing to postulate an age-dependent Poisson failure process and Gamma priors on the mean failure rates at each age, then the probability of r_m failures in a particular subsystem in a time interval T at age m is

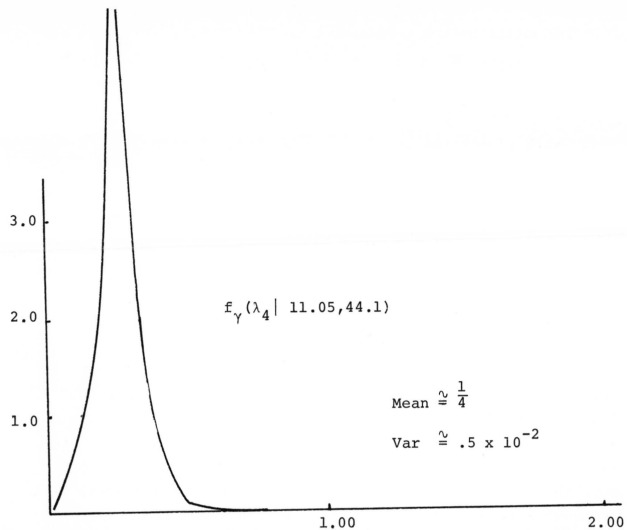

$$f_\gamma(\lambda_4 \mid 11.05, 44.1)$$

$$\text{Mean} \cong \frac{1}{4}$$

$$\text{Var} \cong .5 \times 10^{-2}$$

FIGURE 5-10   DISTRIBUTION ON λ_4 AFTER OBSERVING 11 FAILURES
IN 44 SHIP YEARS OF OPERATION

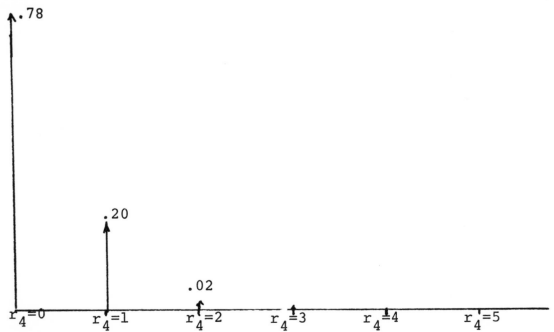

FIGURE 5-11 DISTRIBUTION ON r_4 AFTER OBSERVING 11 FAILURES IN 44
SHIP YEARS OF OPERATION

163

$$P(r_m \mid m) = \frac{T^{r_m} t_m'^{r_m'} (r_m + r_m' - 1)!}{r_m! (r_m' - 1)! (T + t_m')^{r_m + r_m'}}$$

This expression holds as long as the interval T is small enough so that the probability of more than one failure in T is insignificant. For most major seagoing components, if one chooses a T of, say, 1/6 a year, the probability of multiple failures in a single interval T will be negligible. r_m' and t_m' are the parameters of the present distribution on the mean failure rate at age m_j. For wishy-washy priors, r_m' is the number of failures observed in t_m' years of operation of the component in question at age m.

In order to develop an algorithm for deciding whether or not a component should be automatically replaced at overhaul and, if so, how often, consider the sequence of points in time $0, T, 2T, 3T, \ldots$ where t = 0 is the launch time of the ship. Let the nth time in this sequence be denoted by t_n. The t_n corresponding to overhaul are assumed to be chosen exogenously, that is, the overhaul schedules are considered to be fixed as is the length of life of the ship. Let $C_S(m)$ be the cost of replacing the component during overhaul if the component is m years old at the time. Let $C_F(m)$ be the expected cost of failure of the component during operation at age m. C_F will be difficult to estimate so, at least in the preliminary development of this algorithm, the program might have to be run parametrically seeing what effect different C_F's have on the resulting replacement policy.

Assuming the DM is an expected value decision-maker we define $W_n(x)$ to be the minimum expected cost of failure and replacement of the component throughout the remainder of life of the ship if at time t_n this component is x T-periods old. We proceed to derive a recursion relationship for the function W_n. If at time t_n the ship is being overhauled, then

164

we have a choice: replace the component or don't. If we don't
replace it, we will incur no immediate costs with respect to
this component and at the next stage, t_{n+1}, that is, at t_n+T,
the component will have aged to x_j+1. The minimum expected
costs from t_{n+1} on of being in this state is by definition
$W_{n+1}(x+1)$. If, on the other hand, we do replace the subsystem,
then we will incur a cost of $C_S(x)$ and at time t_{n+1} the component will be only 1 T-period old. The minimum expected cost
from t_{n+1} on of being in this state is $W_{n+1}(1)$. Thus, if we
are in overhaul at t_n, $W_n(x)$ is given by

$$W_n(x) = \text{minimum} \begin{cases} W_{n+1}(x+1) \\ \\ C_S(x) + W_{n+1}(1) \end{cases}$$

This expression assumes no failure is possible between t_n and
t_{n+1}. Generally, the ship will be in overhaul for at least one
T. If the ship is operating at t_n, then the expression for
$W_n(x)$ takes on different form. In this case at t_n, we have no
discretionary decisions, we can only wait and see if a failure
at t_{n+1} we will be in state $x+1$; if it does, then we will have
to bear the costs of replacement out of overhaul and at t_{n+1}
the age of the replaced system will be 1.

The expectation of the value of the best we can do in each
of these two instances is $W_n(x)$ or

$$W_n(x) = P(0|x) \cdot W_{n+1}(x+1) + P(1|x) \cdot (C_F(x) + W_{n+1}(1))$$

where the P's are given by the first equation in this section.
For any such component the table $W_n(x)$ and the corresponding
optimal replacement policy can be computed by observing that at
the projected scrapping date of the ship, t_{NMAX}, $W_{NMAX}(x)$ equals
0 for all x since no further costs will be incurred after the
ship is scrapped. This boundary condition can be substituted

into the r.h.s. of the relevant expression for W_{NMAX-1} and we can proceed to tabulate W_n by backwards recursion using the second to the last expression if t_n is an overhaul time and the last expression if it is not.

The input to this algorithm then is:

1) The projected overhaul schedule of the ship through its life--which t_n's correspond to in-overhaul;

2) The costs of replacement in overhaul and the expected costs of failure outside of overhaul, $C_S(m)$ and $C_F(m)$;

3) The failure history of the component under analysis as described by the number of failures which have been observed in the component at each age and the size of the sample for each age, the r_m's and t_m's. Notice that the algorithm is not adaptive in the sense that when a failure occurs during the process it doesn't change its ideas about the probabilities in the same way that the boiler tube pulling program did. Since the experimentation in this problem is not discretionary as it was in the tube pulling case, this omission will not be serious, especially if we rerun the whole algorithm periodically, incorporating the latest failure data.

The algorithm as outlined has been programmed and is quite inexpensive to run, since the state space is very small.* For each subsystem so analyzed, the output of the program is a table indicating for each possible subsystem age at each overhaul time whether or not the subsystem should be automatically replaced. The program also outputs the optimal value function which gives the future expected replacement/failure costs associated with following the expected cost minimizing policy.

---

*The program is available from the M.I.T. Department of Ocean Engineering.

166

5.7 THE COST OF FAILURE AS A RANDOM VARIABLE*

In failure problems, the DM not only does not know the parameters of the process generating the times of the failures, but also he does not know the parameters generating the cost of each failure. This problem can also be treated in a Bayesian manner by assuming:

1) The cost of an individual failure is generated by a probabilistic process with unknown parameters;

2) Specifying priors on the unknown parameters; and

3) Using Bayes Rules to update these distributions as failure cost data becomes available.

For example, one might be willing to assume that the loss due to the kth failure of subsystem j, x_{jk}, is generated by a Normal process with unknown mean and variance in which case, if one assumes a Normal prior on the mean and a Gamma prior on the Variance, then all the relevant distributions can be calculated without difficulty. The analysis is presented in reference 18, Chapter 11. In short, as above one can develop the distribution on the cost of the kth failure, x_{jk}, of each subsystem $j, h_j(x_{jk})$ which is consistent with the DM's cost of failure data and his prior feelings and one can update this distribution in a mechanical manner.

Such distributions will allow us to address situations in which the choice of a major subsystem depends critically on the DM's feelings about the reliability and maintenance costs of the alternatives but the DM has little or no failure data on at least some of the alternatives. The classic example of this type of problem is whether or not to go with a newly-developed main propulsion system.

Before we can speak to such decisions, we must distinguish between two types of failures:

---

*This section assumes somewhat more background in probability than the earlier ones and can be skipped without loss in continuity.

1) Those in which the subsystem which fails is effectively replaced; that is, the effective age of the subsystem is zero immediately after repair;

2) Those in which the subsystem is merely repaired--brought back to the state it was in before the failure with no reduction in effective age. For subsystems of the second type, one can obtain the distribution of the loss in any year due to j subsystem failures by convolution. Let $g(x_j|a)$ be the distribution of the total loss due to failures of component j in year a of the life of the ship where j is a component subject to Type 2) failures.

Since

$$
y_j = \begin{cases} 0 \text{ if } r_{aj} = 0 \\ \\ x_{j1}+x_{j2}+\ldots x_{jr_{aj}} \quad \text{for } r_{aj} > 0 \end{cases}
$$

where r_{aj} is the number of failures of subsystem j in year a. Under the assumption that the distributions on the x_{jk}'s are the same and that the amounts lost on each occurrence of a failure of j are independent, then $g(y_j|a)r_{aj}$ times, and then summing the results over r_{aj} weighted by $P(r_{aj}|a)$. Then the expected annual cost of failures of component j, given that the relevant component is a years old is

$$
\bar{C}_j(a) = \sum_{Y_j} y_j g(y_j|a)
$$

Now, if the useful life of the ship is L years, then the present value of expected cost of j failures over the life of the ship is simply:

$$
\bar{T}_j(L) = \sum_{a=0}^{L} \rho^a C_j(a)
$$

where ρ is the discount rate. The distribution of the total loss is simply the L-fold convolution of $g(y_j|a)$ with a running from 0 to L.

The second type of repair in which the effective age of the component is reduced to 0 presents a slightly more difficult problem, for in this case we have a renewal process. To simplify the discussion, let us assume that the probability of more than one failure of this type of subsystem in a year is negligibly small. (This assumption can easily be relaxed.)

One approach to the problem of determining the expected loss from failures of this type of subsystem through time is through the relevant renewal equation. However, a related but much more instructive approach is to proceed as follows. Let a be the age of the ship. Then, for all a such that $0 \leq a \leq L$ define $_jW_a(m)$ to be the expected cost of failures of component j for the remainder of the life of the ship, given that the ship is presently a years old and component j is m years old. $_jW_L(m) = 0$, for if a = L the ship is retired and no future costs can be experienced. For a <L the function $_jW_a(m)$ obeys the following recursion.

$$_jW_a(m) = \begin{cases} P(0|m) \cdot W_{a+1}(m+1) \\ \\ +P(1|m) \cdot [(\sum_{x_j} g(x_j|m) \cdot x_h + _jW_{a+1}(1)] \end{cases}$$

This equation merely says the expected failure cost in the future of the component at age m, given that the ship is a years old equals the similar cost of the system at age a+1 a year from now if no failures occur, weighted by the probability of no failure in year a plus the sum of the expected cost of failure in the future of the replaced system (weighted in year a).* Thus, the top line of the r.h.s. refers to the event "no failure

---

*Discounted expected cost will be obtained if the future failure costs are multiplied by the discount rate.

in year n" while the bottom line refers to the event "failure in year n."

The probabilities in the above recursion are known at this point. Therefore, we can solve for $_jW_a(m)$ in the following manner. Starting at a = L-1 substitute $_jW_L(m)$ into the right-hand side. The left-hand side will then be $_jW_{L-1}(m)$ which in turn can be substituted in the right-hand side and $_jW_{L-2}(m)$ determined. Continue this process until n=0 is reached. $_jW_0(0)$ then is the expected cost of j type failures for a new ship. In other words, $_jW_0(0) = \bar{T}_j(L)$ for those subsystems for which a repair is tantamount to replacement.

We are now in a position to speak to the problem of including failure costs in investment decisions. The total lifetime expected costs due to mechanical failure of a particular ship (say, diesel) is simply

$$\sum_j T_j(L)$$
over all subsystems j

This sum can be included in the other costs associated with this ship and the results compared with the similar quantity for the other alternatives (say, steam). Insofar as the DM is an expected value decision-maker, he should choose that alternative which results in the minimum present valued expected costs.

CHAPTER 6

SEARCH AND EXPLORATION PROBLEMS

Of course, not all marine decisions under uncertainty involve vessel employment and acquisition or hardware maintenance and replacement. An extremely important set of problems arises in search and exploration. The sea is a uniquely opaque medium. The problem of finding anything under the sea surface, whether it be a lost submarine or a mineral or oil deposit, is correspondingly difficult. The resultant costs are high and sometimes astronomical and uncertainty piles on uncertainty. In this chapter, we will barely begin to dip our toes into the sea of challenging search problems with which the marine environment confronts us.

We will start by discussing a problem in which our uncertainties concerning the location of the searched-for object and our uncertainties about the effectiveness of our search sensors take on a particularly well-structured form, then we will move to the general problem of oil and mineral exploration at sea.

6.1   THE PALOMARES PROBLEM

On the morning of January 17, 1966, a B-52 on a routine training flight was taking on fuel from a KC-135, 32,000 feet above the Spanish Mediterranean coast when both planes suddenly caught fire and crashed on the coastline near the town of Palomares. Four hydrogen bombs were aboard the B-52, three of which were quickly located on land. The fourth bomb could not be found and was presumed to be somewhere offshore. An undersea search for this weapon was mounted.

Due to the highly sensitive nature of the bomb, it was considered mandatory to either retrieve the device or to somehow determine that it was extremely unlikely that unfriendly interests could locate and retrieve the object. The question then facing the U.S. government and ultimately the President was: how long should they search for the object without finding it before the above criterion would, in some sense, be satisfied?

171

There are *two* sets of uncertainties related to this type
of search problem:

1) The DM is uncertain where the object is;

2) The DM is uncertain as to how effective his search
    sensors will be in locating this particular object.

The second set of uncertainties is not only a product of
uncertainties as to the characteristics of the sensor but, much
more importantly, of uncertainties with respect to the characteristics of the *in situ* target. Is the bomb intact? What is
its orientation? Is it wedged in a crevasse? Is it buried in
mud or sitting atop a smooth bottom, etc.? The key to the solution of this type of problem is in keeping the two interrelated
sets of probabilities straight.

Let us consider the locational uncertainties first. In the
Palomares problem, since the point of collision was reasonably
well established, from the physics of the problem one could
delineate a region into which the committee assigned the responsibility for managing the search was willing the stipulate the
bomb must have fallen. This region encompassed a portion of the
shoreline and a roughly fan-shaped portion of the shelf. Let
us divide the region into an arbitrary number of areas
$\{A_m: m=1,2,...M\}$ based on geographical characteristics relating
to search effectiveness.

This partition of the region should be chosen so that *a
priori* each area is roughly homogenous with respect to sensor
effectiveness. For now, we shall assume that there is only
one sensor applicable to a particular area. Further, we will
assume that for each area, one can define what one means by a
"look" on that area. A look may consist of a chain of men walk-
ing down the beach or a complicated sonar search pattern. It
doesn't matter as long as what we mean by a look in each area
is well defined.*

---

*The determination of efficient "looks" or area search patterns
 is an interesting subproblem of long standing. See references
 8 and 15.

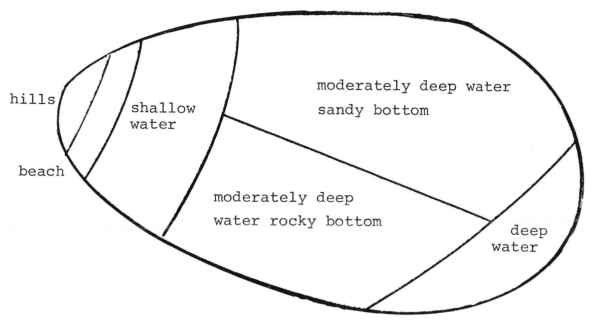

HYPOTHETICAL PARTITION OF REGION
FIGURE 6-1

6.2 DEVELOPMENT OF DETECTION PROBABILITIES

Let L_m be the event that the object is actually located in area m. The first step in tackling this problem is to develop a prior distribution on where the object is, a distribution on the events $\{L_m:m=1,...M\}$. Let $f_m^O=Pr(L_m)$ be this distribution. This is by necessity a subjective distribution representing the DM's feelings about whatever knowledge about the accident he has prior to any search. As such, it could be obtained by Bayesian decision theoretic introspection as outlined in Chapter 2. In the case at hand, the problem was turned over to a committee of experts. Therefore, a mechanism had to be evolved for arriving at a prior which the committee could collectively agree was consistent with the prior information relating to the location of the bomb. The committee evolved the following procedure for making sure that the investigators had incorporated all their prior knowledge about the accident into the prior and incorporated it in an internally consistent manner.

A number of possible scenarios or reconstructions of the accident were postulated such as:

1) Device stayed with main part of plane's fuselage.

173

2) Device separated immediately from plane at point of impact and fell.

3) Device separated immediately from plane, deployed parachute and fell. And so on.

In all about ten mutually exclusive and collectively exhaustive hypotheses were developed. For each such hypothesis, it was a relatively simple matter to use the physics of the postulated scenario to develop noncontroversial distributions on the point of location of the device *conditional on the scenarios actually having taken place*. Call these probabilities $p(x,y|z)$: $p(x,y|z)$ is the probability that the device is located at point (x,y) if scenario z actually occurred. Having developed these conditional distributions, the various experts involved sat down and argued among themselves until they reached agreement on an unconditional distribution $p(z)$ representing the probability that scenario z had in fact happened. At this point they had the required prior, for by the Sum Rule:

$$f_m^o = \int_{(x,y) \in A_m} \sum_z p(x,y|z) p(z)$$

In short, by breaking the prior into an "objective" conditional distribution and transferring all "subjective" judgments to a single variable, a prior which a number of people could agree upon was derived. This device can often be used to advantage in developing priors which incorporate all our prior knowledge in a consistent manner whether or not a committee is involved.*

The second set of uncertainties involves the effectiveness

---

*From a Bayesian point of view, perhaps the most significant point of the whole Palomares incident is that it illustrates that subjective probabilities have been used and accepted at the highest level of decision-making in the U.S.A. When DM's are faced with a critical problem where uncertainty is obviously crucial, biases against attempts to deal with uncertainty systematically can quickly disappear.

174

of the search. We need to know p_m, the probability that we will find the object on the next look in m *given that the object is actually in* m. Unfortunately, we can't be sure of p_m. It will depend, among other things we can't know for certain, on the exact location and condition of the object and its immediate surroundings. In short, p_m is an unknown and, therefore, as Bayesians, it has a distribution function. Let $g_m^o(p_m)$ be its distribution. Since p_m is a probability the natural choice for the form of this distribution, as we saw in Chapter 5, is a Beta. Therefore, assume with little loss in generality that this prior is a member of the Beta family of distributions. Let the prior parameters of this Beta be r_m' and n_m'. That is,

$$g_m^o(p_m) = f_\beta(p_m | r_m', n_m')$$

In an actual problem, (r_m', n_m') would be derived from detailed operational studies of the effectiveness of the sensor in A_m, given the search pattern chosen for A_m and the physical characteristics of this area.*

At this point we must make a critically important assumption. We must assume that our feelings about sensor effectiveness in a particular area m are unaffected by what we learn about sensor effectiveness in any other area m_o. Strictly speaking, this would be true only if our uncertainties regarding the effectiveness of our sensor in a particular area were solely due to uncertainties regarding the target and its background, and further that the backgrounds are independent. Even if we choose our areas judiciously this will hardly ever be true, but given a sensor with which we have considerable experience, any

---

*It will generally be wise at this point to repartition the search region so that each area is roughly homogeneous with respect to *both* prior sensor effectiveness and prior probability of being located into this area. Such repartitioning can lead to less costly searches. Since in the problem at hand cost was a very secondary consideration, it will simplify the exposition if we stay with the original partitioning.

dependencies will generally be weak. Further, for the problem
at hand, the independence assumption is conservative in the
sense that any dependencies would result in a shorter search
before the cut-off point is reached if they were taken into
account. Nonetheless, this is an important enabling assumption
and there will be situations where it is untenable and the following analysis will be inappropriate.

Let F_m^n be the event that the object is found on the nth
look in area m and let $F_m^{n'}$ be the complementary event. That
is, $F_m^{n'}$ is the event "object not found in first n looks in area m."
Given a distribution on p_m, the probability that we find the
object on the first look in m *given that the object is located
in m* is given by:

$$Pr(F_m^1 | L_m) = \int_{p_m} Pr(F_m^1 | L_m p_m) \cdot Pr(p_m)$$

$$= \int_{p_m} p_m \cdot g_m^o(p_m)$$

That is, the probability of finding the object on the first look
in m, given that it's there, is equal to the mean of the initial
distribution on p_m. If we start out with a Beta prior with
parameters (r_m', n_m') then this expression simplifies to:

$$Pr(F_m^1 | L_m) = \mu_\beta(r_m', n_m') = r_m'/n_m'$$

We are now in a position to collect all the relevant probabilities at the beginning of the search.

$$Pr(L_m) = f_m^o \qquad\qquad Pr(L_m') = 1 - f_m^o$$

$$Pr(F_m^1 | L_m) = \mu_\beta(r_m', n_m') \qquad Pr(F_m^{1'} | L_m) = 1 - \mu_\beta(r_m', n_m')$$

$$Pr(F_m^1) = f_m^1 \cdot \mu_\beta(r_m', n_m') \qquad Pr(F_m^{1'}) = 1 - f_m^o \mu_\beta(r_m', n_m')$$

The first question we ask ourselves is: how should we adjust
our probability on the object's being in m, given that we have

looked there and didn't find it? That is, what is $Pr(L_m - F_{m'}^1)$
which we will denote by f_m? In general, f_m will denote the
present probability that the object is in area m , given the pattern of looks prior to the present and that we have yet to find
the object. By Bayes Rule,

$$Pr(L \mid F_m^{1'}) = \frac{Pr(F_m^{1'} \mid L_m) Pr(L_m)}{Pr(F_m^{1'})}$$

$$f_m = \frac{(1 - \mu_\beta(r_m', n_m')) \cdot f_m^O}{1 - \mu_\beta(r_m', n_m') f_m^O}$$

$$= \frac{(n_m' - r_m') \cdot f_m^O}{n_m' - r_m' \cdot f_m^O}$$

As common sense and the above expression indicated $f_m < f_m^O$.
But we know that the object is somewhere in the region or
$\sum_m Pr(L_m) = 1$ where $Pr(L_m)$ is our present probability on the
objects being in m. Thus, when we decrease the probability of
the objects being in m we must renormalize the probabilities
on the objects being located in the other areas accordingly.
These renormalized values can also be obtained by Bayes Rule:

For any $m_o \neq m$

$$f_{m_o} = Pr(L_{m_o} \mid F_m^{1'}) = \frac{Pr(F_m^{1'} \mid L_{m_o}) Pr(L_{m_o})}{Pr(F_m^{1'})}$$

$$= \frac{1 \cdot Pr(L_{m_o})}{1 - \mu_\beta('_m, n_m') f_m^O}$$

$$= \frac{f_{m_o}^O}{1 - (r_m'/n_m') f_m^O}$$

where the superscript o's should now be taken to mean "old" probability, that is, the locational probabilities obtaining before the most recent look.*

If we take a look in a particular area m and fail to find the object, we must adjust not only our probability on the object's being in m but also our feelings about the effectiveness of our search sensors in the particular area. So the next question is: how do we adjust our feelings about search effectiveness, given that we have taken a look in m and didn't find anything? In this respect, we are interested in three probabilities:

1. $Pr(F_m^2|F_m^{1'})$, the probability of finding the object on the second look in m, given that we didn't find it on the first.

2. $Pr(F_m^2|F_m^{1'}L_m)$, the probability of finding it on the second look in m, given that we didn't find it on the first and it is there.

---

*In the actual historical analysis of the Palomares problem, this renormalization was not done. As a result the f_m's over all areas became smaller than an exogenously selected number, the likelihood of ever finding the object was argued to be small enough so that the search could safely be abandoned. The analysis went awry at this point. Fortunately, the form of the error was such that the conclusions might be said to be generally correct, although the decision-maker was certainly misled as to the basis on which he was making the cut-off decision. In any event, no damage was done since the object was located before the cut-off point was reached. In the subsequent search for the submarine Scorpion, the renormalization was done, but then one had no "criterion" for cutting off the search.

3. $g_m(p_m|F_m^{1'}L_m)$, the probability that the likelihood of finding the object in m on the next look is p_m, given that we didn't find it on the first look in m and it is there. In short, we want the posterior distribution on p_m after not finding the object on the first look in m.

The first of these three probabilities is related to the second and our new (present) probability on the object's being located in m, f_m, by

$$Pr(F_m^2|F_m^{1'}) = Pr(F_m^2|F_m^{1'}L_m)Pr(L_m|F_m^{1'}) + Pr(F_m^2|F_m^{1'}L_m')Pr(L_m'|F_m^{1'})$$

$$= Pr(F_m^2|F_m^{1'}L_m) \cdot f_m$$

We will denote this probability by h_m. More generally, h_m is the present probability we will find the object on the next look in area m, given the pattern of looks up to the present.

The second probability is related to the third by

$$Pr(F_m^2|F_m^{1'}L_m) = \int_0^1 p_m \cdot g_m(p_m|F_m^{1'}L_m)dp_m$$

which is merely a restatement of the result that the probability of finding the object in the next look in m, given it is there, is equal to the mean of our present distribution on p_m. Finally, the third distribution can be obtained by Bayes Rule

$$g_m(p_m|F_m^{1'}L_m) = \frac{Pr(F_m^{1'}|p_mL_m)g_m^o(p_m)}{\int\limits_{p_m} Pr(F_m^{1'}|p_mL_m)g_m^o(p_m)}$$

Substituting in our Beta prior, we obtain

$$g_m(p_m | F_m^{1'} L_m) = \frac{(1-p_m) f_\beta (p_m | r_m', n_m')}{\int\limits_{p_m} (1-p_m) f_\beta (p_m | r_m', n_m')}$$

$$= \frac{(1-p_m) \cdot (B(r_m', n_m')^{-1}) \cdot (1-p_m)^{n_m'-r_m'-1}}{\int\limits_0^1 (1-p_m) \cdot (B(r_m', n_m'))^{-1} \cdot p_m^{r_m'-1} \cdot (1-p_m)^{n_m'-r_m'-1} dp_m}$$

$$= \frac{p_m^{r_m'-1} \cdot (1-p_m)^{n_m'+1-r_m'-1}}{B(r_m', n_m'+1)}$$

$$= f_\beta (p_m | r_m', n_m'+1)$$

The posterior distribution on p_m after an unsuccessful look in m is a Beta distribution with parameters $(r_m', n_m'+1)$. In general, after n_m unsuccessful looks in area m, the distribution on p_m will be a Beta with parameters $(r_m', n_m'+n_m)$. Notice that this distribution is not affected by the probability that the object is actually in m nor by the results of any looks taken outside of m. This is a product of our definition of p_m to be the probability of finding the object on the next look in m *given that it's there* and our assumed lack of dependence between sensor effectiveness in area m and sensor effectiveness in any other area.

Given the above result we note that the probability of finding the object in area m on the next look, given that it's there and we have already had n looks in this area, is the mean of a Beta with parameters $(r_m', n_m'+n_m)$ or $r_m'/(n_m'+n_m)$. Thus, the probability of finding the object in m, given that it's there, decreases inversely with the number of looks we have already taken at m.

6.3 SEARCH CUT-OFF CRITERION

We are now in a position to speak to the problem of determining a cut-off point for the search. In order to do so, we will have to assume a search strategy. If differentials in the cost of taking a look in area m as opposed to taking a look in some other area are insignificant or at least small, one obvious strategy is to always take your next look in the area which has the highest current probability of discovery, h_m, i.e., the highest $r'_m \cdot f_m (n'_m + n_m)^{-1}$.. This strategy will maximize the probability of discovery in any finite number of total looks, N. If we use this strategy, it is a relatively simple matter to calculate the probability of discovery within N looks for any N.*

The probability of no discovery in N looks, H(N), can be recursively obtained by simulating the search process H(0)=1.0. Start the simulation by beginning with that area which has the highest $h_m^O = m_\beta (r'_m, n'_m) f_m^O$. Say it's m*, then H(1)=H(0)(1.-h_{m*}^O). Assume no luck. Calculate new h_m's for each area using the relations given above. Pick area which now has the highest h_m, say, m**. H(2)=H(1)·(1-h_{m**}). Assume no success. Calculate new h_m's. Pick area which has highest h_m; say, m***. H(3)=H(2)·(1-h_{m***}). Continue in this recursive manner as long as desired. In general, H(N+1)=H(N)·(1-$h_{m*** \ldots ***}$).

$$\longleftarrow N+1 \longrightarrow$$

Having calculated H(N) for all N of interest, it is a simple matter to obtain H(N|J), the conditional probability of not finding the object on the next N looks given that we have already performed J looks and not found it. By the definition of conditonal probability:

$$H(N|J) = \frac{H(N+J)}{H(J)}$$

for H(N+J) is the probability of the joint event "no discovery in first J looks and no discovery in next N looks."

H(N|J) will be an increasing function of J due to the monotonic decrease in the probabilities of finding the object on the next look in an area, given that it's there. That is, the longer we look without finding the object, the higher the prob-

---

*The following recursive procedure works equally well for any completely defined search policy.

ability that we will not find it in the next N looks.

The two-dimensional table H(N|J) will allow us to establish a cut-off for the search. To do this we ask the decision-maker to prescribe a combination of number of looks by unfriendly forces and a probability of no discovery in this number of looks which he wants to exceed. For example, he may say search until he finds it or the probability of not finding it in the next 1000 looks is greater than .999. The decision-maker is tacitly assuming that the unfriendly forces have the same sensors and the same priors as we do. Substituting the decision-maker's requirements of N=1000 and H(1000|J)>.999. We would search H(1000|J) for the lowest J such that the corresponding H(1000|J) exceeded .999. This should be the length of our search if we are to be consistent with this statement of the problem. Of course, the indicated J could be 0 in which case we shouldn't search at all. This is not a necessarily unreasonable possibility, but it does hint at one of the defects in the above problem statement. The costs of search and the costs of having unfriendly types find the bomb which is the real trade-off involved have never been made explicit. Clearly, if the above methodology is to be made useful for any but the most internationally sensitive searches, means for incorporating the relevant cost functions into the analysis will have to be developed. Some preliminary ideas in this direction are developed in the following section.

6.4 ALGORITHMS FOR ALLOCATING SEARCH EFFORT

If the number of areas in a Palomares type search is quite small, for example, three, then it is possible to develop dynamic programs for solving several variants of the search allocation problem. The most straightforward such algorithm speaks to the situation where the searcher's preference function depends only on the cost of the search and whether or not the object is found. That is, we do not have the "what if the other side finds it?" problem. Let $\pi(X,C)$ be such a preference function where X=1 if object is found and X=0 if object is not found and C is the cost of the search. Let C_m be the cost of a single look in area m. A Bayesian will attempt to maximize his expected preference so define $W_n(n_1,n_2)$ to be the maximum expected prefence associated with the search attainable if we have already made n_1 looks in area 1, n_2 looks in area 2 and $n-n_1-n_2$ looks in area 3. Such a pattern of looks implies that we have already spent $n_1C_1+n_2C_2 +(n-n_1-n_2)C_3$ on the search. Thus, W_n obeys the following recursion:

$$W_n(n_1,n_2)=\text{maximum} \begin{cases} \pi(0,C) & \text{(stop the search)} \\ & \text{(look in area 1)} \\ h_1 \cdot \pi(1,C+C_1)+1-h_1) \cdot W_{n+1}(n_1+1,n_2) \\ & \text{(look in area 2)} \\ h_2 \cdot \pi(2,C+C_2)+(1-h_2) \cdot W_{n+1}(n_1,n_2+1) \\ & \text{(look in area 3)} \\ h_3 \cdot \pi(1,C+C_3)+(1-h_3) \cdot W_{n+1}(n_1,n_2) \end{cases}$$

where $C=n_1C_1+n_2C_2+(n-n_1-n_2)C_3$ and h_m is as defined in the preceding analysis. In order to get the computation started, pick a number of looks, K, which is large enough so that one can be sure if the search lasts this long it should not be con- tinued. Then $W_K(n_1,n_2)=\pi(0,n_1C_1+n_2C_2+I-n_1-n_2)C_3)$. Depending on the choice of K and what is a reasonable maximum on the number of looks in any particular area for the problem at hand, searches with three, four, or possibly five different areas will be computationally feasible via this algorithm.*

If the DM is worried about the other side, then one possible approach is to expand his preference function to include this worry. Let $\pi(1,C)$ be as before, but assume that if the search ends without discovery the DM's preference depends on

---

*The above recursion, of course, assumes a three-area search. The equivalent four- and five-area algorithms can be obtained by adding a state variable for each additional area.

a) The cost of the search;

b) The probability that the other side will not find the object in the next N looks, $H(N|$given pattern of looks up to now). Let $\pi(H,C)$ be this preference function. In this case, the above algorithm is unaltered except for the first line in the right-hand side which becomes $\pi(H(N|$pattern up to now$),C)$ where H can be calculated at each stage and state by assuming that the other side follows the probability of discovery maximizing search outlined in the last section, given the various probabilities obtaining at this stage and state.

The above formulation of the problem puts a heavy onus on the DM to come up with a preference function. He may simply prefer to throw up his hands and say, "Here is C dollars, give me the search that maximizes the probability of discovery within this budget." In which case, define $W_n(n_1,n_2)$ to be the maximum probability of discovery attainable, given that we have already looked n_1 times in area 1, n_2 times in area 2, and $(n-n_1-n_n)$ times in area 3 without finding the object. Then

$$W_n(n_1,n_2) = \text{maximum}\{h_m \cdot 1 + (1-h_m) \cdot W_{n+1}(n_1',n_2')$$

where n_1' equals n_1+1 if m=1 and n_1 otherwise, $n_2'=n_2+1$ if m=2 and n_2 otherwise, and the maximum is taken over all m such that $n_1 C_1 + n_2 C_2 + (n-n_1-n_2)C_3 + C_m \leq C_0$. If no m meets this test, then $W_n(n_1,n_2)=0$. Start computation with an n high enough so that one can be sure no m meets the test.

By solving the above algorithm for a range of budgets, C_0, one obtains the cost-effectiveness curve for the problem, i.e., the maximum probability of detection that can be obtained for a given budget.* For each of the cost-effective strategies it is an easy matter to calculate the $H(N|$pattern of search) for the strategy. This function along with the cost-effective curve

---

*Or equivalent to the minimum budget needed to obtain a specified level of the preference function.

can then be presented to the decision-maker and he can, by applying his preferences directly to the set of cost-effective strategies, decide on a budget. Often DMs have a much easier time with the latter kind of decisions than they do with developing multidimensional preference functions.

6.5 THE OFFSHORE OIL DECISION TREE

Presently five billion dollars a year is being spent in the search for and development of offshore oil and gas fields. The individual investments adding up to this figure are being made in the face of grave uncertainties concerning how much oil/ gas will be found, if any, and how much it will cost to locate and discover whatever resources are there. Obviously, offshore petroleum exploration decisions represent a worthy subject for our techniques. Unfortunately, they are so difficult that we will be able to make only a little progress towards their solution. However, the importance of these decisions makes even a little progress at least mildly interesting.

It is not difficult to draw up a segment of the decision tree facing the offshore operator contemplating exploration of an as-yet-undeveloped area. At present, there are only two useful means of obtaining data concerning the offshore oil resources in a particular area: seismic tests and drilling. Hence, in dealing with an individual locale the offshore oil operator is faced with what may be regarded loosely as a two-stage decision:

1) Whether or not to run a seismic survey in a particular area;

2) Following this decision and the results, if any, whether or not to drill in the area. A decision tree describing this sequence is shown in Figure 6.2.

The cost of a seismic survey offshore can run a million dollars; a single offshore oilwell can cost two to three million dollars. The tree shown does not allow for the uncertainties with respect to these costs, but concentrates solely on the uncertainties with respect to the seismic results and the results

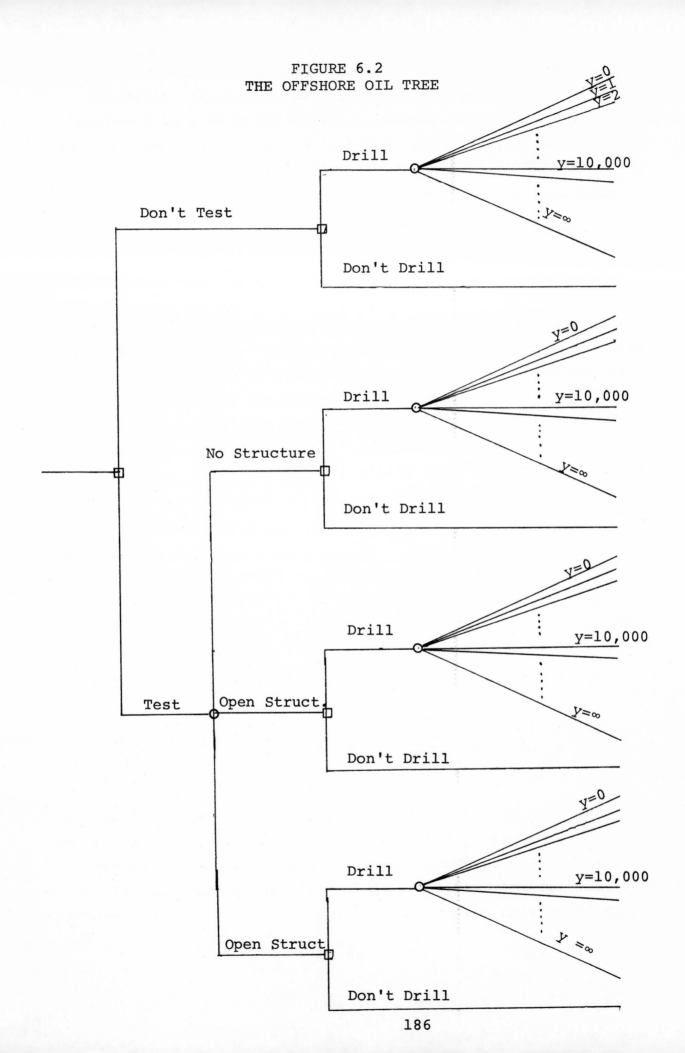

FIGURE 6.2
THE OFFSHORE OIL TREE

186

of the drilling.

Seismic tests result in a pattern of returns revealing (some of the) density changes in the subseabottom rock. This pattern is interpreted by a geologist for structures associated with oil deposits. In Figure 6.2 we have abstracted the results of this process by assuming the geologist distinguishes only three categories of results: no structure (NS), open structure (OS), closed structure (CS).

In general, closed structure is more likely to yield petroleum than an open structure which, in turn, is more favorable than no structure. In actual fact, a geologist's discrimination process is much more refined than this. However, let us at least start with this three-way category. The number of kinds of seismic results can be expanded as desired. Call the test results x, i.e., x equals either NS, OS or CS.

An exploratory well results in a flow (hopefully) and core analyses from which a petroleum engineer estimates the number of recoverable barrels (cubic feet) in the reservoir located, if any. We have called this random variable y in the figure.

Given such a tree, there are two sets of probabilities with which the DM must be concerned:

1) $\Pr(y|x)$, the conditional probability on the number of recoverable barrels, given the test results;

2) $\Pr(x)$, the probability of obtaining a particular test result.

If the DM knew these probabilities for all possible values of y and x, he could assign them to the relevant branches in his tree, apply his preference function to the tips of each path in the tree, and fold the tree back in the standard manner. In general, of course, the DM has no way of knowing these probabilities with certainty. Therefore, as a Bayesian he will have to regard these probabilities as random variables and set up a sampling process for developing and updating distributions on these unknowns.

6.6   A BAYESIAN SAMPLING PROCESS FOR Pr(y|x)

We will begin by developing a Bayesian sampling process aimed at the probability of recoverable reserves amounting to y given a particular test outcome, i.e., conditional on a particular x. Since all the probabilities in this section will be conditional on this particular x, we will suppress this conditioning event in the notation. In the next section, we will consider the distributions on the test results, Pr(x).

1)   The postulation of a sampling process which process is described by a set of conditional probabilities on the possible outcomes of the sample, Pr(outcome|underlying state of Nature). In Joe's case the underlying state of Nature was either "a peach" or "a lemon" and the conditional probabilities were Pr(test outcome|P) and Pr(test outcome|L) for all possible test outcomes. In Chapter 5, the unknown underlying state of Nature was characterized by parameter(s) of a specified density function such as the mean rate of failure, λ, in a Poisson process or the p in the Bernoulli process.

2)   The development of subjective distributions on the unknown state of Nature. These distributions were called priors.

3)   The use of Bayes Rule to obtain a new distribution of the unknown state of Nature after having observed a particular test outcome. We saw that this calculation was considerably simplified if the form of the prior was chosen to match the form of the sampling distribution, in which case we said we had a conjugate prior.

In the problem at hand, y is the amount of recoverable reserves obtained in a single well. Hence y is certainly non-negative but, as wildcatters well know, just as certainly has a finite probability of being zero--a dry hole. Conditional on x, the density function on y might have a form such as that shown in Figure 6.3, with a spike at y = 0 and some continuous unimodal density function for y's greater than 0.

The question is: what would be a reasonable functional form

FIGURE 6.3

HYPOTHETICAL DENSITY FUNCTION
ON RECOVERABLE RESERVES LOCATED

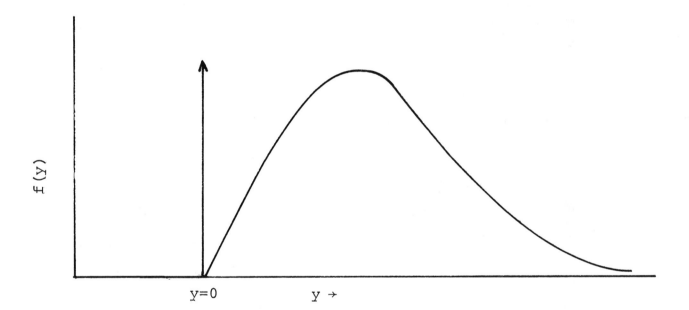

189

to assume for this density function? Kaufman, reference 6, has argued that a Lognormal distribution might do the job and reference 6 presents some empirical data to back up this contention as well as an argument based on the Lognormal as the central limit of a multiplicative process. However, the evidence is not too convincing in the sense that a large number of other functional forms could also be made to fit the data, and further it is not clear in what sense the sedimentary processes leading to petrochemical formations are multiplicative. Another set of sampling functions which are at least as flexible as the Lognormal and which have the practical merit that we have already seen them are the Gamma density functions. Thus, this section is going to investigate the possibility of a sampling process in which the probability of actually obtaining reserves of x barrels, given that we have observed a particular seismic outcome, say, Open Structure, is

$$
f(y|p,\lambda,r) = \begin{cases} p & \text{for } y = 0 \\[2em] (1-p) \cdot \dfrac{e^{-\lambda y}(\lambda y)^{r-1}}{(r-1)!} & \text{for } y > 0 \end{cases}
$$

where p, λ, and r are the unknown parameters describing the state of Nature, given the seismic return OS.*

One can develop a pseudogeological argument for choosing this particular functional form. To wit, with a certain probability p Nature chose to collect no sedimentary deposits at the drilling location. If, on the other hand, she did choose to make such deposits, the length of the sedimentary periods and hence the recoverable reserves obtaining from each such period was determined by a Poisson process of parameter λ. The number of such periods was r. This argument derives from the fact that the sum of r time periods resulting from a Poisson process is

---

*As mentioned earlier, in this section we are suppressing the argument x. In other words, written out in full this density function is $f(y|p(x),\lambda(x),r(x))$. We will have one such density function for each possible seismic outcome.

distributed according to the above Gamma. While this scenario bears a faint resemblence to geological reality, it is, like Kaufman's argument for the Lognormal, hardly convincing. The basic and more important point is that this is a very flexible three-parameter family which can be made to fit just about any having the general characteristics of Figure 6.5.

Step 2 in developing a Bayesian sampling process involves the postulation of prior on the unknown states of Nature, in this case, on the parameters p, λ, and r. Let us regard the sampling process as sequential in the sense that, when we obtain a y after drilling, we first ask: was the well dry or not? If the answer is No, then we ask: how large was y? This sequential viewpoint is sketched in Figure 6.4. Viewed in this manner, it is clear that the conjugate prior for p is a Beta for, at the first question, we have a simple Bernoulli process with only two possible outcomes either defective (dry hole) or not--the same kind of process we had in the boiler tube pulling problem. Further, if the Beta prior on p is $f_\beta(p|n_d',n')$ then by the arguments in Chapter 5, after having observed n_d dry holes in n attempts given seismic result x, the posterior on p is $f_\beta(p|n_d'+n_d,n+n')$ and the probability that y=0 is the respective Betabinomial.

Given the above sequential viewpoint, we can regard the Gamma part of the above density as the conditional probability of y given y>0. With respect to λ and r and parameters of this Gamma we have three possible cases:

1) r known, λ unknown

2) r unknown, λ known

3) r unknown, λ unknown

Actually, the third case is the only one we are really interested in, but for pedagogic purposes we want to sneak up on it gradually.

The first case is quite similar to the situation facing us in the automatic replacement problem and as in the automatic

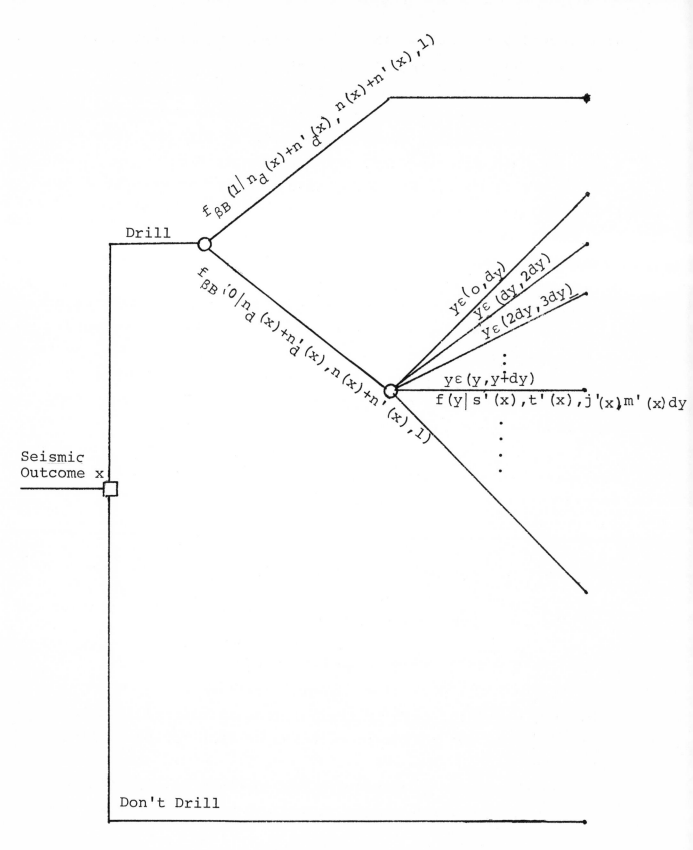

FIGURE 6.4

BLOW UP OF THAT PORTION OF OFFSHORE OIL
TREE CONDITIONAL ON SEISMIC OUTCOME x

replacement problem the conjugate prior on λ is a Gamma. For suppose we postulate such a prior on $\lambda, f_\gamma(\lambda|s',m')$ and then observe a result y>0. By Bayes Rule

$$f(\lambda|y,1,s',m') = \frac{\dfrac{e^{-\lambda y}(\lambda y)^{r-1}\lambda}{(r-1)!}\dfrac{e^{\lambda s'}(\lambda s')^{m'}s'}{(m'-1)!}}{\dfrac{\displaystyle\int_0^\infty e^{-\lambda y}(\lambda y)^{r-1}\lambda\ e^{-\lambda s'}\lambda s'^{m'}s'd\lambda}{(r-1)!\qquad (m'-1)!}}$$

$$= \frac{e^{-\lambda(y+s')}\lambda^{r+m'-1}}{\displaystyle\int_0^\infty e^{-\lambda(y+s')}\lambda^{r+m'-1}}$$

$$= \frac{e^{-\lambda(y+s')}\lambda^{r+m'-1}}{\dfrac{(r+m'-1)!}{(y+s')^{r+m'}}}$$

$$= f_\gamma(\lambda|y+s',r+m')$$

Notice that each time we get a wet hole after having observed the seismic result to which this density applies we up the second parameter m' by the (assumed for now) known r. Hence, after a large number of wells have been drilled given x, the second parameter will be approximately the number of wet holes times r.

If case 2 obtains--λ known but r unknown--then we must postulate a prior on r. The secret to picking a conjugate prior is to pick a density function which *as a function of the unknown parameter* looks like a generalization of the sampling distribution regarded as a function of the same parameter. From the point of view of r, the Gamma sampling density has the form

$$\frac{C(\lambda y)^{r-1}}{(r-1)!}$$

where $C = e^{-\lambda y}\lambda$ is a constant as far as r is concerned. Hence, we postulate a prior of the form

$$f(r|t',j') = \frac{(t')^{r-1}}{C(t',j')((r-1)!)^{j'}}$$

where r is restricted to the positive integers since we know
y>0. (Remember r can be interpreted as the number of sedimentary eras leading to the deposit.)   In the above expression

$$C(t',j') = \sum_{r=1}^{\infty} \frac{(t')^{r-1}}{((r-1)!)^{j'}}$$

is a normalization factor such that the density function sums
to 1.00 over all possible r. Notice it depends only on the
parameters of the density function and not r. We shall call
this family of distributions the hyperPoisson density denoted
$f_{hP}(r|t',j')$.

   The posterior on r after having observed a y>0 in a single
well is given by

$$f(r|y,1,t',j') = \frac{\dfrac{e^{-\lambda y}(\lambda y)^{r-1}}{(r-1)!} \cdot \dfrac{t'^{r-1}}{C(t',j')((r-1)!)^{j'}}}{\sum\limits_{r=1}^{\infty} \dfrac{e^{-\lambda y}(\lambda y)^{r-1}\lambda}{(r-1)!} \dfrac{t'^{r-1}}{C(t',j')((r-1)!)^{j'}}}$$

$$= \frac{\dfrac{(\lambda y t')^{r-1}}{((r-1)!)^{j'+1}}}{\sum\limits_{r=1}^{\infty} \dfrac{(\lambda y t')^{r-1}}{((r-1)!)^{j'+1}}} = \frac{(\lambda y t')^{r-1}}{((\lambda y t',j'+1)((r-1)!)^{j'+1}}$$

$$= f_{hP}(r|\lambda y t',j'+1)$$

which proves that the hyperPoisson is the desired conjugate
prior. Notice that y and t' combine in a multiplicative manner
increasing the first parameter if y is greater than the (assumed)
known mean of the process, λ^{-1}, and smaller otherwise.

The second parameter increases by one with each relevant drilling and hence after many such wells will approximately equal the number of wet holes drilled after observing seismic result x.

As usual, the denominator in Bayes Rules is just the probability of the conditioning event. Hence, in this case

$$\sum_{r=1}^{\infty} \frac{e^{-\lambda y}(\lambda y)^{r-1}\lambda t'^{r-1}}{((r-1)!)^{j'+1}C(t',j')}$$

equals the probability of observing recoverable reserves of y on the next wet hole drilled after observing x if the present updated parameters of the distribution on r are t' and j', which we will call $Pr(y|\lambda,t',j')$.

$C(t',1)$ is simply $e^{t'}$ and $f_{hP}(r|t',1)$ is the familiar Poisson, hence the name hyperPoisson. $C(t',2) = I_0((2t')^{1/2})$ where I_0 is the zeroth order modified Bessels function of the first kind. The higher order C's have not been given names, but since they converge extremely rapidly computation is no problem.

The real-life situation in which neither λ nor r are known is slightly messier. In this case, we must postulate a joint conjugate prior on the pair of random variables, (λ,r). Such a density function is the following four-parameter prior:

$$f(\lambda,r|s',t',j',m') = \frac{e^{-s\lambda}\lambda^{m'(r-1)+j'-1}s^{j'}t'^{r-1}}{((r-1)!)^{j'}C(s',t'j',m')}$$

where

$$C(s',t',j',m') = \sum_{r=1}^{\infty}\int_{o}^{\infty} \frac{e^{-s'\lambda}\lambda^{m!(r-1)+j'-1}s'^{j'}t'^{r-1}d\lambda}{((r-1)!)^{j'}}$$

To show that this function is a conjugate prior, assume a single sample yields y>0.

195

$$f(\lambda,r|y,1,s',t',j',m') = \cfrac{\cfrac{e^{-\lambda y}(\lambda y)^{r-1}\lambda}{(r-1)!}\; \cfrac{e^{-s'\lambda}\lambda^{m'(r-1)+j'-1}s'^{j'}t'^{r-1}}{((r-1)!)^{j'}C(s',t',j',m')}}{\displaystyle\sum_{r=1}^{\infty}\int_0^{\infty}\cfrac{e^{-\lambda y}(\lambda y)^{r-1}\lambda}{(r-1)!}\; \cfrac{e^{-s'\lambda}\lambda^{m'(r-1)+j'-1}s'^{j'}t'^{r-1}}{((r-1)!)^{j'}C(s',t',j',m')}d\lambda}$$

$$= \cfrac{\cfrac{e^{-\lambda(y+s')}\lambda^{(m'+1)(r-1)+(j'+1)-1}(yt')^{r-1}}{((r-1)!)^{j'+1}}}{\displaystyle\sum_{r=1}^{\infty}\cfrac{(t'y)^{r-1}}{((r-1)!)^{j'+1}}\int_0^{\infty}e^{-\lambda(y+s')}\lambda^{(m'+1)(r-1)+(j'+1)-1}d\lambda}$$

$$= \cfrac{\cfrac{e^{-\lambda(y+s')}\lambda^{(m'+1)(r-1)+(j'+1)-1}(yt')^{r-1}}{((r-1)!)^{j'+1}}}{\displaystyle\sum_{r=1}^{\infty}\cfrac{(t'y)^{r-1}}{((r-1)!)^{j'+1}}\;\cfrac{((m'+1)(r-1)+(j'+1)-1)!}{(y+s')^{(m'+1)(r-1)+(j'+1)}}}$$

$$= \cfrac{e^{-\lambda(y+s')}\lambda^{(m'+1)(r-1)+(j'+1)-1}(y+s')^{j'+1}(yt')^{r-1}}{((r-1)!)^{j'+1}\,C(y+s',t'y,j'+1,m'+1)}$$

$$= f(\lambda,r|y+s',t'y,j'+1,m'+1)$$

where we can be sure that the constant in the denominator is
of the same functional form as the C(s',t',j',m') since the
entire expression summed over both λ and r is 1.00 (because
Bayes Rule preserves the basic normalization of probabilities)
and the numerator is of the same functional form as the prior.
In short, this prior is a conjugate prior to the Gamma sampling
function when both parameters are unknown. Notice that despite
the long-winded expressions, the combination of the prior parameters with the data is of the simplest possible form. Notice
also that both j' and m' will increase one with each relevant
drilling so that after a reasonably large number of such wells
are drilled they will both be approximately equal to the number
of wet holes drilled after observing seismic result x. If j'
is assumed equal to m', then the above expressions can be sim-

196

plified considerably. The author hesitates to give a name to
the above prior, but it might be called the Gamma-hyperPoisson
since it is a mixture of these two densities. As usual, the denominator in Bayes Rule is the probability of the conditioning
event. Hence, given that the present parameters of the distribution on λ and r having observed seismic result x are
$(s'(x),t'(x),j'(x),m'(x))$, then the probability of a wet hole's
yielding y barrels after seismic result x is

$$f(y \mid s'(x),t'(x),j'(x),m'(x)) =$$

$$= \sum_{r=1}^{\infty} \int_{0}^{\infty} \frac{e^{-\lambda y}(\lambda y)^{r-1}e^{-s'(x)\lambda}\lambda^{m'(x)(r-1)+j'(x)-1}s'(x)^{j'(x)}t'(x)^{r-1}dx}{((r-1)!)^{j'(x)+1}((s'(x),t'(x),j'(x),m'(x))}$$

These are the probabilities we need for the wildcatter's decision
tree. There will be one such distribution for each possible
seismic outcome, x. With the probabilities developed in this
section we can assign the requisite probabilities to the portion
of the offshore operator's tree which follows a particular seismic result. Such a subtree and the indicated assignments are
shown in Figure 6.4.

6.7 THE UNCONDITIONAL PROBABILITIES ON x

In order to complete our assignment of the probabilities to
the tree of Figure 6.2, we need the unconditional probabilities
on each of the possible seismic outcomes. Once again we will
have to postulate a sampling process and develop a prior distribution on the parameters of this process. We have assumed the
number of possible seismic outcomes is finite--in fact, we have
talked as if there were only three, No Structure, Open Structure, and Closed Structure. However, we can as easily develop
the argument for any finite number of outcomes. Suppose the
geologist separates seismic results into K categories and let
the event 'result is in category k' be denoted by x_k.

In this situation, the natural sampling process to assume
is the Multinomial. The Multinomial process with K possible out-

197

comes is characterized by a K-1 paramenter family of density functions. Let n_k be the number of times x_k is observed in $n = \sum_{k=1}^{K} n_k$ trials. If we are dealing with a Multinomial process, the probability that x_1 occurs n_1 times, x_2 occurs n_2 times, etc., is

$$f_\beta(n_1,n_2,\ldots,n_k \mid p_1,p_2,\ldots p_k) = \frac{n! \prod\limits_{k=1}^{K} p_k^{n_k}}{\prod\limits_{k=1}^{K} n_k!}$$

where the p_k's, the parameters of the process, are such that $\sum_{k=1}^{K} p_k = 1.00$. This is a straightforward generalization of the Bernoulli process for situations in which there are more than two possible outcomes. The p_k's can, of course, be interpreted as the probability with which Nature picks the kth outcome. Of course, we don't know what Nature's p_k's are so we have to postulate a prior on them. The conjugate prior in this case is the Vector Beta which is given by

$$f_\beta(p_1,p_2,\ldots p_k \mid n'_1,n'_2,\ldots,n'_K) = \frac{(\sum\limits_{k=1}^{K} n'_k)! \prod\limits_{k=1}^{K} p_k^{n'_k}}{\prod\limits_{k=1}^{K} n'_k!}$$

Notice how the form of f_β has been chosen to match the form of f_M. It is almost obvious from this match and can easily be shown that the posterior on $(p_1,p_2,\ldots p_K)$ after having observed n_1 occurrences of x_1, n_2 occurrences of x_2, and so on is*

$$f_\beta(p_1,p_2,\ldots,p_k \mid n_1+n'_1,n_2+n'_2,\ldots,n_k+n'_k)$$

---

*Reference 12 generalizes this argument to the case where one has a set of unknown vectors of the form $(p_1,p_2\ldots p_K)$ as one does in a Markov process with unknown transition probabilities. For this situation, there exists a straightforward generalization of the Vector Beta known as the Matrix Beta which serves as a conjugate prior. Through the Matrix Beta, a Bayesian can develop his probabilities concerning a Markov Process about which he has limited information. A case in point are the transition probabilities required by our first formulation of the vessel employment problem in Chapter 4.

Given that the current, *updated* parameters on $(p_1, p_2 \ldots p_K)$ are $(n_1', n_2', \ldots, n_K')$ then the probability of outcome x_k on the next test is

$$\Pr(x_k) = \int\limits_{p_k} p_k \int\limits_{p_{k'\neq k}} \ldots \int f_\beta(p_1, p_2, \ldots p_K | n_1', n_2' \ldots n_K')$$

It is easily shown (see reference 12, Chapter 6) that the inner multiple integral which equals the marginal density of p_k is an ordinary Beta with parameters $(n_k, \sum_{k=1}^{K} n_k)$. Thus, the above expression implies that the desired probability is the mean of this marginal density or

$$\Pr(x_k | n_1', n_2' \ldots n_K') = \frac{n_k'}{\sum\limits_{k=1}^{K} n_k'}$$

Thus, for large numbers of trials or wishy-washy priors, this probability will be approximately equal to the ratio of the number of times result x_k has been observed to the total number of tests. In any event, if we keep track of the number of times each result has been observed we are in a position to assign probabilities to the leftmost set of chance branches in Figure 6.2.

6.8   THE NO TEST OPTION

Seismic tests are expensive and can often yield very little information. Thus, the operator will certainly want to analyze the option of drilling without tests just as Joe had to consider the option of not having the yard look at his ship, which option in fact turned out to be Joe's best move when we analyze his problem using a non-EMVing preference function. The probabilities associated with the no-test option are not independent of the probabilities we have already derived. What is required for this portion of the tree are the probabilities of the various possible y's unconditional on the test results. But by the Sum Rule

$$\Pr(y) = \sum\limits_{k=1}^{K} \Pr(y | x_k) \Pr(x_k)$$

199

and we have just derived both sets of probabilities on the right-hand side of this expression. In short, our assignment of the probabilities to the tree of Figure 6.2 is complete.

6.9 SUMMARY

We have seen that, under this formulation, the operator's state at any time can be described by the following *updated* parameters:

1) $(n_1', n_2', \ldots, n_K')$ where n_k' is the number of times he has observed seismic result k plus his original prior parameters on p_k.

2) For each x_k, k=1,2,...K,

   a) $n_d'(x_k), n_w'(x_k)$, the number of dry holes and wet holes drilled after observing x_k plus the original prior values of these parameters.

   b) $s'(x_k)$, $t'(x_k)$, $j'(x_k)$, $m'(x_k)$, the sum of the recoverable reserves obtained from wet holes drilled after observing x_k plus the original prior value of the first parameter, the product of the recoverable reserves obtained from wet holes drilled after observing x_k times the original prior value of this parameter, the number of wet holes drilled after x_k plus the original prior value of the second to the last parameter, and again the number of wet holes drilled after x_k plus the original prior value of the last parameter.

Even allowing for redundancies in the above list, the number of state variables required to describe the operator's position at any time is approximately twelve even if only three possible seismic categories are allowed, so dynamic programming of the coupled drilling decision is out. This is a tough, complex problem. It will not admit of easy solutions. Even the rather complicated formulation described above is highly unrealistic in many aspects and it treats each drilling decision somewhat in

200

isolation. However, such complexity is a two-edged sword. It
implies that the unaided intellect will also have a very difficult time of integrating all the relevant data and coming up with
decisions consistent with the DM's desires. In such cases, it
may well pay the DM to study the results of making even some
rather unrealistic assumptions to see where they lead him. The
insight that results, while not determinant, will often be worth
far more than its cost in which case the decisions will be improved, and that is the name of the game. Of course, this will
not always be the case. The decision as to whether or not to try
Bayesian analysis in a particular situation is itself amenable
to Bayesian analysis. However, before we get into an infinite
regress we had better call it quits.

REFERENCES

1. Bellman, R., "Adaptive Control Processes: A Guided Tour." New Jersey: Princeton University Press, 1961.

2. Bellman, R. and Dreyfus, S., "Applied Dynamic Programming." New Jersey: Princeton University Press, 1962.

3. Devanney, J. and Lassiter, J., "The Martingale Tanker Market Model." M.I.T. Commodity Transportation Laboratory. Unpublished Working Paper, 1971.

4. Drake, A. W., "Fundamentals of Applied Probability Theory." New York: McGraw-Hill, 1967.

5. Grayson, C. J., Jr., "Decisions Under Uncertainty--Drilling Decisions by Oil and Gas Operators." Boston: Harvard University Press, 1960.

6. Kaufman, G., "Statistical Decision and Related Techniques in Oil and Gas Exploration." New Jersey: Prentice-Hall, 1963.

7. Kelly, J., "A New Interpretation of Information Rate." Bell System Technical Journal, Vol. 35, 1956, pp. 917-926.

8. Koopman, B., "The Theory of Search." Operations Research, Vol. 4., No. 3, June 1956, pp. 324-346.

9. Koopmans, T. C., "Tanker Freight Rates and Tankship Building," Haarlem, Netherlands, 1939.

10. Lorange, P. and Norman, V., "Risk Preference Patterns among Scandivanivan Tankship Owners." Institute for Shipping Research, Bergen, 1970.

11. Lorange, P. and Norman, V., "Risk Preference and Strategic Decision Making in Large Scandinavian Shipping Enterprises." Institute for Shipping Research, Bergen, 1971.

12. Martin, J. J., "Bayesian Decision Problems and Markov Chains." New York: John Wiley, 1951.

13. Morse, P. M. and Kimball, G. E., "Methods of Operations Research." New York: John Wiley, 1951.

14. Mossin, J., "An Optimal Policy for Lay-Up Decisions." Swedish Journal of Economics, 1968, p. 1970.

15. Pratt, J. W., "Risk Adversion in the Small and in the Large." Econometrica, Vol. 32, No. 1-2, Jan.-April 1964, p. 122.

16. Pratt, J., Raiffa, H. and Schlaifer, R., "Introduction to Statistical Decision Theory." New York: McGraw-Hill, 1965.

17. Raiffa, H., "Decision Analysis--Introductory Lectures Under Uncertainty." Reading, Mass.: Addison-Wesley, 1968.

18. Raiffa, H. and Schlaifer, R., "Applied Statistical Decision Theory." New York: McGraw-Hill, 1965.

19. Svendsen, A. A., "Factors Determining the Laying-Up of Ships." Shipbuilding and Shipping Record, June 19, 1958, p. 805.

20. Von Neumann, J. and Morgenstern, O., "Theory of Games and Economic Behavior." New Jersey: Princeton University Press, 1944.

21. Woodyard, Alan, "Dynamic Programming of a Charter Market Model." M.I.T., Master's Thesis, Department of Ocean Engineering, 1971.

22. Zannetos, Z., "The Theory of Oil Tankship Rates." Cambridge: M.I.T. Press, 1966.

23. Zoller, D., "The Tanker Order Decision." M.I.T. Commodity Transportation Laboratory. Unpublished Working Paper, 1970.